THE LITTLE BOOK OF

POPULAR PERENNIALS

THE LITTLE BOOK OF

POPULAR PERENNIALS

A GUIDE TO THE SELECTION AND CULTIVATION OF YOUR FAVOURITE PLANTS

Maureen Little

SPRING HILL

For
my perennial friends
Alyson, Val and Tricia

Published by Spring Hill, an imprint of How To Books Ltd.
Spring Hill House, Spring Hill Road
Begbroke, Oxford OX5 1RX
United Kingdom
Tel: (01865) 375794
Fax: (01865) 379162
info@howtobooks.co.uk
www.howtobooks.co.uk

First published 2013

British Library Cataloguing in Publication Data
A catalogue record of this book is available from the British Library.

ISBN: 978 1 905862 90 0

Produced for How To Books by Deer Park Productions, Tavistock, Devon
Designed and typeset by Mousemat Design Ltd
Printed and bound by Graficas Cems, Villatuerta (Spain)

Contents

Acknowledgements 7
Introduction 8

A to Z of 100 Popular Perennials 13

Acanthus 15
Achillea 17
Aconitum 19
Actaea 21
Agapanthus 23
Agastache 25
Ajuga 27
Alchemilla 29
Allium 31
Alstroemeria 33
Anchusa 35
Anemone 37
Anthemis 39
Aquilegia 41
Artemisia 43
Aster 45
Astilbe 47
Astrantia 49
Bergenia 51
Brunnera 53
Campanula 55
Centaurea 57
Centranthus 59
Chrysanthemum 61
Cirsium 63
Clematis 65
Convallaria 67
Coreopsis 69
Corydalis 71
Crocosmia 73
Dahlia 75
Delphinium 77
Dianthus 79
Dicentra 81
Dierama 83
Digitalis 85
Doronicum 87
Echinacea 89
Echinops 91
Epimedium 93
Eremurus 95
Erigeron 97
Eryngium 99
Eupatorium 101
Euphorbia 103
Filipendula 105
Foeniculum 107
Gaillardia 109
Gaura 111
Geranium 113
Geum 115
Helenium 117

Helleborus 119
Hemerocallis 121
Heuchera 123
Hosta 125
Iris – bearded 127
Iris – beardless 129
Knautia 131
Kniphofia 133
Lamium 135
Lathyrus 137
Lavandula 139
Leucanthemum 141
Liatris 143
Ligularia 145
Lobelia 147
Lupinus 149
Lysimachia 151
Malva 153
Monarda 155
Nepeta 157
Origanum 159
Paeonia 161
Papaver 163
Penstemon 165
Perovskia 167
Persicaria 169
Phlomis 171
Phlox 173
Polemonium 175
Polygonatum 177
Potentilla 179
Primula 181
Pulmonaria 183
Ranunculus 185
Rudbeckia 187
Salvia 189
Scabiosa 191
Sedum 193
Sidalcea 195
Solidago 197
Stachys 199
Thalictrum 201
Verbascum 203
Verbena 205
Veronica 207
Veronicastrum 209
Viola 211
Zantedeschia 213

Appendices
1. Main flowering season – in order of season 214
2. Main flowering season – in alphabetical order of perennial 216
3. Perennials for different places and purposes 220
4. Perennials which may be harmful 224
5. Index of common names of plants and their Latin equivalent 225
Glossary 228
Useful Addresses and Websites 232
Index 233

Acknowledgements

Once again I am indebted to my relatives and friends for their inspiration and encouragement. A big bouquet to all of them, especially:

Georg, my husband, who provides much-needed and constant love and assistance in the background: he is very much the woven hazel support to my clump of delphinium – take him away and I would soon collapse! Becca and James – without whose love I would soon wither.

Giles Lewis and Nikki Read at Spring Hill Publishers who continue to nurture my budding writing career.

Tricia Brown, my dear friend and fellow plantaholic, who owns The Garden Studio where I go to 'play in the soil'!

Toady: if it hadn't been for that first chapter, the writing seed would never have been sown, let alone been given the chance to germinate.

Introduction

I suppose you could have a garden without herbaceous perennials but I rather think that it would be like having a roast beef dinner with no Yorkshire puddings, or a Punch and Judy show without Judy – all right as far as it goes, but lacking that vital ingredient. Whereas trees and shrubs provide focal points and a framework to the garden, it is the herbaceous perennials that give us the main thrust of colour, texture, form and interest throughout the seasons. They are both the stalwarts and the divas of the garden.

Add to that the fact that many herbaceous perennials have fragrant flowers, that even more attract a whole range of insects, and that they are relatively easy to grow and maintain, then there is really no excuse for not including them in a planting scheme.

What are herbaceous perennials?

Let's look at the first part – the 'herbaceous' bit. In a nutshell, herbaceous plants are those with non-woody stems. The term includes plants whose above-ground growth dies back in winter, and also non-woody, evergreen plants that may retain some growth during the dormant period.

'Perennial' is applied to plants that live for more than two years. Put those two terms together and we come up with non-woody plants that live for more than two years. These are the types of plants that this book is about. Much of the time, however, the 'herbaceous' part is dropped, so when gardeners talk about their perennials, they invariably mean their herbaceous perennials, like *Aster*, *Campanula* or *Sedum*.

My selection of 100 popular perennials

The plants I have selected for my top 100 are just that – a selection. I have tried to be as objective as I can, and I consulted my friend who owns a specialist wholesale and retail plant nursery as to which perennials she and her wholesale customers find are the most popular. I also spoke to other nursery owners at plant events and flower shows, and contacted a number of garden centres to find out which are their 'best sellers'. Inevitably, though, the final decision as to what is included and what is left out has been my subjective choice, and if your favourite perennial is not included, apologies.

What is included in this book

This book is really about herbaceous perennials, but I have taken a slight liberty and included some plants that aren't strictly classified as herbaceous, but in practical gardening terms are treated as such. *Perovskia*, for example, a sub-shrub, is so at home in the herbaceous border that it would be churlish of me not to include it.

What I have tried to do in this book is to include as much basic information about each of the chosen perennials, in as concise a form as possible, to act as an easy reference. If you want to know the best way to propagate *Echinacea*, or find out whether *Nepeta* is best grown in sun or shade, for example, you will find the answer in each respective entry. If any detail is lacking, I apologize; if there are mistakes, they are entirely my own.

In further explanation, here is a sample entry.

Aconitum

(ak-o-*ni*-tum) (Common name – Monkshood, Wolfsbane) (Family – Ranunculaceae)

The heading gives the species name, followed by the pronunciation – the stressed syllable is shown in italics. Any common name follows, and then the family to which the plant belongs.

Type of plant Hardy, deciduous

The type of plant tells you whether or not it is hardy (see Glossary) and whether it is evergreen or deciduous.

Height/Spread Up to 1.5m/50cm, depending on species

The height and spread of a species can vary enormously, so the maximum dimensions at maturity are given.

Flowers/Foliage Spikes of blue, violet, occasionally white, pink or yellow, hooded flowers late spring to late autumn, depending on species/Round, lobed, dark green leaves

This is a brief description of the form, colour and flowering times of the flowers, followed by a brief description of the foliage.

Best growing conditions Sun or dappled shade; rich, moisture retentive soil

This tells you which position the plant is happiest in and what type of soil it likes. You can take it as read that plants are generally happiest in neutral soil, unless information is given to the contrary.

Longevity Approximately 4 years

This is the average maximum life of the plant, after which it will need dividing or discarding. Some perennials last only three years, others much longer, depending on the plant itself and the conditions in which it is grown.

Propagation Division, early spring

This tells you what the best method is to increase your stock and when (but see the section on plant breeder's rights, below).

Maintenance/Problems Deadhead flowers regularly; cut down plants in late autumn; tall varieties may need staking/Usually trouble-free

Here you will find concise information about how to maintain your plant to keep it looking good, what sort of pests and diseases are most likely to affect it, and if there are any other problems you should be aware of.

Good for Cutting, bees

This tells you what you can use the plant/flowers for – other than looking pretty in the garden!

Looks good with *Hemerocallis, Phlox, Veronicastrum*

This is quite subjective, but here you will find suggestions about what each perennial looks good alongside.

Selected varieties/cvs *Aconitum* 'Spark's Variety'* – violet blue; *A.* 'Stainless Steel' – silvery blue; *A.* x cammarum 'Pink Sensation' – shell pink; *A.* 'Bressingham Spire'* – violet blue

My selected varieties and cultivars are, again, a very subjective choice. I have included ones that I like and/or those that have proven to be good garden plants. Those marked with an asterisk (*) have been awarded a Royal Horticultural Society's Award of Garden Merit (see below).

☠ **BEWARE** ☠ All parts of the plant are toxic; can cause skin irritation
If this section is included, take care when dealing with the plant in question, for the reasons stated.

Some perennials really deserve a separate volume of their own to do them justice and my meagre efforts may fall short on many occasions, but I hope there is enough information to at least give you a basic insight and overall impression of each of the plants.

Plant entries also include some extra material that I hope you will find interesting: this ranges from episodes in my own horticultural experience, tried and tested tips, to gobbets of information that don't fall into any particular category.

What is not included

Paradoxically, although I have included some plants that aren't strictly herbaceous perennials, I have excluded two groups of plants that are part of this grouping, namely grasses, and (with a few notable exceptions) bulbs, tubers and rhizomes. Each of these, I think, deserves a volume of its own.

I have not included detailed information about various gardening techniques, terms, pests and diseases. There are some brief explanations in the Glossary, but there are many excellent books and websites on specific topics which go into the areas in much more depth than I am able to here. A really good starting point is the website of the RHS (www.rhs.org.uk).

Universal jobs

Some jobs are universal, irrespective of the type of plant you are dealing with. All plants will benefit from a good mulch of organic matter in spring or autumn; they will appreciate not having to compete with weeds; and if we have a particularly dry spell, you may find that you need to water, albeit judiciously, plants that show signs of stress. These jobs are not included in the maintenance entry.

Royal Horticultural Society's Award of Garden Merit

Next to some of the selected varieties you will see an asterisk (*). This indicates that the plant has been granted the Award of Garden Merit (AGM) by the Royal Horticultural Society (RHS). In a nutshell, it means that the plant is considered garden-worthy – the full criteria can be found on the RHS's website (www.rhs.org.uk). Be aware, though, that if a plant hasn't been granted an AGM this doesn't mean that you shouldn't grow it. There are thousands, if not millions, of perennials available to gardeners, so only a certain number can be trialled and assessed each year. Use your judgement: if you like a plant, have a go at growing it – assuming that the aspect and soil conditions are suitable, of course! But if you really have no idea which ones to go for, look for the AGM and at least you will know that one of the most prestigious horticultural societies in the world thinks that the plants are worthwhile.

Plant breeder's rights

You may come across this term or its abbreviation, PBR, on plant labels in garden centres and nurseries. This means that the breeder of the particular plant has a form of intellectual property rights over it, preventing anyone from benefiting from propagating it, selling it, and so on, without the breeder's authority. So beware – do not take cuttings, divide it, and so on, even to give to friends.

Hardiness

For the most part, all the perennials I have chosen are hardy in the British Isles (zones 8a or 8b). Information is given in each entry for those that are not.

Latin names

In all cases I have given the Latin name of the plant, followed by the common name where there is one. The reason for using Latin names is that common names for plants can vary from region to region (a bluebell in Scotland is not the same as a bluebell in England, for example), so knowing the proper, undisputed Latin name is invaluable, especially when it comes to looking for plants in a nursery or online. You will find a list of common names of plants and their Latin equivalent in Appendix 5 towards the end of the book.

Latin pronunciation

I have also included a guide to the pronunciation of the Latin name. The part of the name that is stressed is shown in italics. I have opted for the most widely used way of articulating the word. I take the general view that as long as the person you are speaking to understands which plant you are talking about, then it doesn't really matter if you say 'toe-mar-toe' and she says 'toe-may-toe'! (But please don't call the whole thing off!)

A to Z of 100 Popular Perennials

Acanthus spinosus

Acanthus

(ak-*an*-thus) (Common name – Bear's breeches) (Family – Acanthaceae)

Type of plant	Hardy, deciduous
Height/Spread	Up to 1.5m/1m, depending on species
Flowers/Foliage	Closely packed hooded flowers in white, green or muted pink-purple in late spring to midsummer/Cut or jagged, sometimes spiny, dark green leaves
Best growing conditions	Sun; well-drained but moisture retentive soil
Longevity	Approximately 4 years
Propagation	Root cuttings, dormant season; division, early spring
Maintenance/Problems	Leave spent flower spikes for overwintering insects/ Powdery mildew; slugs; snails
Good for	Cutting – beware spiny leaves on some varieties
Looks good with	*Phlomis*, *Astrantia*
Selected varieties/cvs	*Acanthus dioscoridis* var. *perringii* – pink; *A. mollis* 'Rue Ledan' – white

Acanthus is one of the most arresting perennial plants to have in the border: what it lacks in vibrant flower colour is more than made up for by its bold, statuesque appearance. Indeed, a stylized acanthus leaf was used as a decorative motif on classical Corinthian columns, and later on furniture, fabrics and jewellery.

In the garden its striking appearance and physical dimensions can overwhelm lesser plants, especially *A. spinosus* (pictured), so pair it with something that can either stand up to it, like *Phlomis*, or contrasts well with it, like *Astrantia*.

It is one of those plants that once you have it in the garden it is very difficult to get rid of. This is because its long roots penetrate deep into the soil – if you decide to dig it up, any portion of root left behind will form a new plant. This can be a bane, but by the same token also a blessing, since it can be propagated easily by root cuttings. The probing roots make it a useful plant to have in areas or at times of low rainfall, because it can draw moisture from depths which shallower rooted plants cannot access.

Achillea 'Martina'

Achillea 'Pretty Belinda'

Achillea

(a-*kill*-e-a) (Common name – Yarrow) (Family – Asteraceae)

Type of plant	Hardy, deciduous or semi-evergreen, depending on species
Height/Spread	Up to 90cm/40–60cm, depending on species
Flowers/Foliage	Flat-topped 'platforms' of small individual cream, yellow, pink, pale lilac, orange or cerise flowers in late spring to autumn, depending on variety/Ferny, grey-green or dark green leaves
Best growing conditions	Sun; well-drained soil
Longevity	Approximately 3 years
Propagation	Cuttings, early summer; division, early autumn
Maintenance/Problems	Deadhead flowers regularly; cut down plants in mid-autumn; divide if centre of plant becomes straggly; may need staking/Powdery mildew
Good for	Cutting, bees
Looks good with	*Allium, Salvia, Lavender, Nepeta, Perovskia*
Selected varieties/cvs	*Achillea* 'Martina'* – yellow; *A.* 'Pretty Belinda' – deep pink; *A.* 'Terracotta' – orange-yellow

There are a multitude of vernacular names for *Achillea*, the most common being yarrow; it is also known as soldier's woundwort, staunchweed and bloodwort, which point to its use as a medicinal herb to heal wounds and staunch the flow of blood. It also has superstitions attached to it; for example, it is said that if you place some under your pillow at night and recite the following poem, you are supposed to dream of your future wife or husband:

> Thou pretty herb of Venus' tree, Thy true name it is Yarrow;
> Now who my bosom friend must be, Pray tell thou me to-morrow.

I can't vouch for its reliability, but stranger things have happened!

Although the flower of the 'wild' *Achillea* is a rather nondescript chalky white colour, the cultivated hybrids have some subtle and striking hues. Most varieties fade in colour as the blooms mature.

If you deadhead regularly new flowers will be produced well into late summer. It is best to cut all the flowering stems back to ground level in mid-autumn, however, to allow the plants to build up before winter sets in.

Aconitum napellus 'Snow White'

Aconitum carmichaelii Wilsonii Group

Aconitum

(ak-o-*ni*-tum) (Common name – Monkshood, Wolfsbane) (Family – Ranunculaceae)

Type of plant	Hardy, deciduous
Height/Spread	Up to 1.5m/50cm, depending on species
Flowers/Foliage	Spikes of blue, violet, occasionally white, pink or yellow, hooded flowers in late spring to late autumn, depending on variety/Round, lobed, dark green leaves
Best growing conditions	Sun or dappled shade; rich, moisture retentive soil
Longevity	Approximately 4 years
Propagation	Division, early spring
Maintenance/Problems	Deadhead flowers regularly; cut down plants in late autumn; tall varieties may need staking/Usually trouble-free
Good for	Cutting (see below), bees
Looks good with	*Hemerocallis*, *Phlox*, *Anemone hupehensis*, *Veronicastrum*
Selected varieties/cvs	*Aconitum* 'Spark's Variety'* – violet blue; *A.* 'Stainless Steel' – silvery blue; *A.* x *cammarum* 'Pink Sensation' – shell pink; *A. carmichaelii* Wilsonii Group – violet blue; *A. napellus* 'Snow White' – white
☠ BEWARE ☠	All parts of the plant are toxic; can cause skin irritation

I have to come clean at this point and admit to my love of *Aconitum*. I have always been fascinated by them – whether it's because of their sinister common name of wolfsbane, or the fact that, being toxic, they have to be treated with the utmost respect, I'm not sure. But I have always felt that their tall spires of shades of blue flowers add a certain presence to a border.

I think their toxicity prevents many garden centres from stocking them and it is true that you have to be very careful when handling them or cutting the flowers – always wear gloves – but this should not prevent us from growing them. If you have trouble growing *Delphinium*, try *Aconitum* instead – they are pretty trouble-free and slugs turn their tentacles up at them.

There are many different varieties available, flowering from as early as May. My favourite is *A.* 'Spark's Variety': it is a very useful addition to the late summer border, with its deep violet-blue flowers that contrast well with the many oranges and yellows that proliferate at this time.

Actaea racemosa

Actaea simplex Atropurpurea Group 'Brunette'

Actaea

(*ak*-tee-a) (Common name – Bugbane) (Family – Ranunculaceae)

Type of plant	Hardy, deciduous
Height/Spread	Up to 1.5m/60cm, depending on species
Flowers/Foliage	Spikes of white, yellow or pink flowers in autumn/Basal green or purple leaves split into leaflets
Best growing conditions	Dappled shade; rich, damp soil
Longevity	Approximately 4 years
Propagation	Division, early spring or autumn
Maintenance/Problems	Cut back in spring/Aphids; slugs; snails
Good for	Shade, back of the border
Looks good with	*Anemone*, *Astilbe*, *Hosta*
Selected varieties/cvs	*Actaea simplex* Atropurpurea Group 'James Compton' – dark green maturing to olive-black foliage, creamy white flowers; *A. simplex* (Atropurpurea Group) 'Brunette' – purple-red leaves, white flushed pink flowers; *A. simplex* 'Prichard's Giant' – green leaves, white flowers
☠ BEWARE ☠	All parts are harmful if ingested; can cause skin irritation

You may find that if you ask for *Actaea* in some garden centres you will be shown a plant named *Cimicifuga*. Don't worry – they are one and the same thing. In 2000 it was discovered that the DNA of both groups was not distinct enough for them to be classified as two, so now they are all called *Actaea*. (Perhaps that's not a bad thing, since *Actaea* is much easier to pronounce than *Cimicifuga*!)

The most popular *Actaea* appear to be those in the Atropurpurea Group. These have foliage of various shades of purple, some verging on black, which appears long before the tall spikes of pale-coloured flowers, making a real statement in the border.

Another species of *Actaea* has useful medicinal properties; this is *A. racemosa* (pictured), otherwise known as black cohosh. It has been found to be helpful in easing the symptoms of the menopause. Be that as it may, it is one of the easiest species to cultivate and makes a good addition to a border in dappled shade.

Agapanthus Headbourne hybrid

Agapanthus

(ag-a-*pan*-thus) (Common name – African lily) (Family – Alliaceae)

Type of plant	Hardy, deciduous or evergreen, depending on species
Height/Spread	Up to 1.5m/60cm, depending on species
Flowers/Foliage	Rounded clusters of funnel-shaped blue or white flowers held on top of leafless stems in mid-summer to mid-autumn, depending on species/Strappy, basal, green leaves
Best growing conditions	Sun; rich, free-draining soil
Longevity	Approximately 5 years
Propagation	Division, early spring
Maintenance/Problems	Deadhead flowers and stems regularly; protect in winter (see below)/Slugs
Good for	Cutting, bees
Looks good with	*Hemerocallis*, *Salvia*
Selected varieties/cvs	*Agapanthus* 'Northern Star' – blue with dark stripe; *A.* 'Double Diamond' – white; *A.* 'Midnight Cascade' – indigo

Agapanthus are one of the most striking of all garden flowers, their globes of flowers rising above their lush green foliage, adding a touch of the exotic to even the most conservative of planting.

Generally speaking, there are two types of agapanthus. First, there are the deciduous ones, like *A.* Headbourne hybrids (pictured), that are usually hardier and can be planted directly in the garden. They will happily live outdoors as long as the soil is free-draining and they are given a protective mulch of bark in the autumn. Second, there are the more-or-less evergreen ones that need frost-free protection over the winter. They are best grown in pots so that they can be taken under cover before the first frosts arrive. Remember to keep watering to a minimum during this time. What the two types both need is a free-draining soil and they will both benefit from a high-potash feed every three or four weeks during the flowering season – this will keep the flowers coming.

My first encounter with *Agapanthus en masse* was in Madeira, where they have colonized the roadsides, much like dandelions do in Britain! There the plants are two-a-penny; well, not quite – more like two-a-euro in the flower market in Funchal!

Agastache 'Black Adder'

Agastache

(ag-as-*ta*-kee) (Common name – Giant hyssop) (Family – Lamiaceae)

Type of plant	Hardy (see below), deciduous
Height/Spread	Up to 1m/40cm
Flowers/Foliage	Dense spikes of tubular blue-purple flowers in mid-summer to early autumn/Egg-shaped, toothed, aromatic green leaves
Best growing conditions	Sun; well-drained, fertile soil
Longevity	Approximately 3 years
Propagation	Division, early spring; semi-ripe cuttings, late summer; seed, spring
Maintenance/Problems	Deadhead flowers and stems regularly; cut back by at least half in autumn/Occasionally powdery mildew
Good for	Cutting, bees, butterflies
Looks good with	*Echinacea*, *Achillea*, *Aster*, *Helenium*
Selected varieties/cvs	*Agastache* 'Black Adder' – blue-violet; *A.* 'Blue Fortune'* – lilac blue

According to my nursery-owning friend, *Agastache* have really only come into their own in the last four or five years, and in that time one variety – *A.* 'Black Adder' – has proved to be the most popular of all. Having seen a bank of this variety growing in the RHS garden at Harlow Carr, alive with butterflies and bees of all descriptions, I can understand why.

Agastache is fairly short-lived as perennials go, but it makes up for it by flowering profusely in its first year. In cold winters it can be borderline hardy, so either mulch the crown with bark or take some cuttings as back-up.

Its form contrasts well with any member of the Asteraceae family, especially the flat daisy-like flowers of *Echinacea* or *Helenium*.

Ajuga reptans

Ajuga reptans 'Atropurpurea'

Ajuga

(a-*ju*-ga) (Common name – Bugle) (Family – Lamiaceae)

Type of plant	Hardy, evergreen
Height/Spread	15–20cm/indefinite
Flowers/Foliage	Spikes of tubular deep blue flowers in summer/Spoon-shaped, green or variegated leaves, depending on species
Best growing conditions	Dappled shade; rich, fairly moist soil
Longevity	Approximately 5 years
Propagation	Division, spring or autumn
Maintenance/Problems	Little maintenance/Occasionally powdery mildew; can be invasive
Good for	Ground cover, bees
Looks good with	Spring bulbs, *Liriope*, *Ophiopogon*
Selected varieties/cvs	*Ajuga reptans* – green leaves, blue flowers; *Ajuga reptans* 'Atropurpurea'– dark purple leaves; *A. reptans* 'Burgundy Glow'– silver-green, flushed red leaves; *A. reptans* 'Catlin's Giant'* – deep bronze-purple leaves; *A. reptans* 'John Pierpoint'– white flowers

Some people might raise an eyebrow at *Ajuga* being included in a book on popular perennials. True, it doesn't have the 'wow' factor of some of the more architectural or colourful species, but it's a good do-er where others would curl up their roots. It actually prefers dappled shade and can cope with all but very dry soil, and it's evergreen to boot.

If you grow it primarily for the leaves, *Ajuga* is a brilliant ground cover plant and provides a wonderful foil for spring-flowering bulbs. The flowers, too, have merit, although they can get a little lost if you grow the variety *A.* 'Burgundy Glow'; the best one for flower contrast is *A.* 'John Pierpoint', which has pure white flowers against glossy, mid-green foliage.

The four most widely available varieties are the first four listed above, but new ones are constantly being introduced. Although it will never be in the 'top ten chart', I predict that this often overlooked plant will start creeping its way into more gardens over the next few years.

Alchemilla mollis

Alchemilla

(al-kem-*il*-la) (Common name – Lady's mantle) (Family – Rosaceae)

Type of plant	Hardy, deciduous
Height/Spread	50cm/50cm
Flowers/Foliage	Clusters of small yellow-green flowers in summer/Round, indented green leaves with serrated edges
Best growing conditions	Sun or part shade; almost any soil
Longevity	Approximately 4 years
Propagation	Division, spring or autumn; seed, spring or autumn
Maintenance/Problems	Prolific self-seeder – deadhead before seed is shed; clear away leaves as they die/Usually trouble free
Good for	Edging, cutting, ground cover
Looks good with	Almost anything!
Selected varieties/cvs	*Alchemilla mollis** – yellow-green; *A. mollis* 'Variegata' – leaves accented with yellow

This unassuming plant has a major drawback: it is such a prolific self-seeder that unless you are scrupulous about deadheading you will find plantlets popping up in the most unexpected – and sometimes annoying – places.

If you can live with that, *Alchemilla* is a very useful plant to have in the garden. The colour of both foliage and flowers complement everything else; it will grow in just about any conditions; and it will cover the ground, smothering weeds, but is not so impenetrable that other plants cannot push their way through.

The frothy flowers look almost ethereal as they appear to hover above the foliage, and the leaves hold on to droplets of water which reflect the light like diamonds – a very nearly magical sight. Indeed, as child I thought that fairies lived in the heart of the plant and came to gather the drops of water when no one was looking!

Although there are a number of species, *A. mollis* is the most widely available. If you don't have it in your garden, there is a good chance that you won't have to buy a plant; ask around the neighbours and you will no doubt find someone only too willing to give you a plant – or ten!

Allium hollandicum 'Purple Sensation'

Allium

(*al*-lee-um) (Common name – Ornamental onion) (Family – Alliaceae)

Type of plant	Hardy bulb
Height/Spread	90cm/15cm
Flowers/Foliage	Globes of individual star-shaped purple or white flowers in summer/Strappy green basal foliage
Best growing conditions	Sun; well-drained soil
Longevity	Approximately 3 years
Propagation	Seed – can take three seasons to flower
Maintenance/Problems	Seed heads can be left on plant over the winter – clear away in spring/Usually trouble-free
Good for	Cutting, bees
Looks good with	*Anemone, Geranium, Salvia, Nepeta*
Selected varieties/cvs	*Allium hollandicum* 'Purple Sensation'* – purple; *A. neapolitanum* Cowanii Group – white; *A. cristophii** – violet-mauve

Technically the name *Allium* refers to a whole host of bulbous plants of the onion family, but here we are looking at the ornamental ones that are grown for their flowers alone. As they are bulbs, I did question as to whether they should be included in this book, but they have become so much a part of the herbaceous border that it seemed nit-picky not to.

Allium seem to have become 'must have' plants in any discerning gardener's patch these days, due in some part to their popularity at the Chelsea Flower Show and other prestigious horticultural events. They pop up there on a regular basis – or should I say 'explode' there, because some do resemble fireworks in mid-display. And in case I'm beginning to sound a little disparaging, let me say that they are one of the 'show garden plants' that do transfer easily to a more modest venue like a back garden.

Allium look stunning when planted between other herbaceous plants in the border, and can act as a unifying punctuation mark, giving a rhythmic coherence to a long border. The foliage can look a little untidy but it is nearly always camouflaged by the plants growing round about to be too much of an eyesore.

Alstroemeria 'Tessa'

Alstroemeria 'White Pink Blush'

Alstroemeria

(al-stro-*meer*-ee-a) (Common name – Peruvian lily) (Family – Alstroemeriaceae)

Type of plant	Hardy, deciduous
Height/Spread	90cm/45cm
Flowers/Foliage	Lily-like flowers in a range of colours in summer/Narrow, twisted green leaves
Best growing conditions	Sun; light, free-draining soil
Longevity	Approximately 3 years
Propagation	Division, spring or late summer – be careful with brittle roots
Maintenance/Problems	Water in dry spells; deadhead regularly; cut back in autumn; mulch over winter/Resent being moved; slugs; snails; aphids; viral infections
Good for	Cutting
Looks good with	*Geranium*, *Nepeta*
Selected varieties/cvs	*Alstroemeria* 'Spitfire'* – bright red with a yellow flash; *A. 'Apollo'** – ivory white with a yellow flash; *A.* 'HRH Princess Alice'* – purplish pink with yellow flash; *A.* 'Tessa' – ruby-red; *A.* 'White Pink Blush – white with pink flash
☠ BEWARE ☠	Can cause skin irritation

Most non-gardeners know *Alstroemeria* as cut flowers wrapped in cellophane in the local supermarket, and indeed their long stems and beautiful, lily-like flowers make them one of the best plants to grow for cutting.

Native to Chile, they can be a little tricky to grow unless you have a sunny site with soil that doesn't hold too much water over winter. Paradoxically, if they have too little water in summer the leaves will turn yellow and the whole plant will die back. It's a balancing act.

Although new, shorter varieties have been introduced, such as the Inticancha Collection, I still like the more statuesque 60cm-plus varieties, of which there are hundreds to choose from. For this reason alone it is worth waiting to buy your plants until they are in flower at the local garden centre or nursery, when you can see exactly what you are getting. Some of the best varieties are given above: if you are a lover of variegation, 'Spitfire' has leaves margined in creamy white.

Anchusa azurea 'Loddon Royalist'

Anchusa

(an-*choo*-za) (Common name – Bugloss) (Family – Boraginaceae)

Type of plant	Hardy, deciduous
Height/Spread	Up to 1.2m/50cm
Flowers/Foliage	Clusters of tubular-shaped blue flowers in summer/Lance-shaped, bristly green leaves
Best growing conditions	Sun; moderately fertile, free-draining soil
Longevity	Approximately 3 years
Propagation	Root cuttings, dormant season
Maintenance/Problems	Deadhead regularly; cut back after flowering/Mildew; mosaic virus
Good for	Bees
Looks good with	*Iris*, *Allium*, *Foeniculum*, *Verbascum*
Selected varieties/cvs	*Anchusa azurea* 'Loddon Royalist'* – blue; *A. azurea* 'Opal' – light blue
☠ **BEWARE** ☠	All parts of the plant are toxic

The blues of *Anchusa* flowers are some of the most beautiful imaginable in the plant world. One of the most arresting sights I have ever seen in a garden was an expanse of gentian-blue *A. azurea* 'Loddon Royalist' through which an orange-peach bearded *Iris* ('Autumn Riesling', I think) was growing: the complementary colours appeared even more intense as the early summer sun drenched the bed.

In garden centres and nurseries you may also come across *A. azurea* 'Dropmore', the oldest known cultivar, which has the same penetrating blue. If you want something a little more subdued, *A. azurea* 'Opal', a shorter-growing variety with light blue flowers, is the one for you.

It's a member of the Borage family so has the same characteristics as the herb – bristly leaves and attractive blue flowers that are magnets for bees and other pollinating insects.

Anchusa is generally known as a very short-lived perennial but it will survive for several years as long as the soil does not retain too much moisture over winter: any hint of over-watering will sound its death knell.

Anemone x *hybrida* 'Honorine Jobert'

Anemone

(an-*em*-o-nee) (Common name – Windflower) (Family – Ranunculaceae)

Type of plant	Hardy, deciduous
Height/Spread	Up to 1.2m/60cm
Flowers/Foliage	Open, saucer-shaped flowers in white, pink, purple-pink, in late summer to autumn/Green leaves with 3 lobes and jagged edges
Best growing conditions	Sun or dappled shade; moderately fertile, free-draining soil
Longevity	Approximately 4 years
Propagation	Division, spring; root cuttings, dormant season
Maintenance/Problems	Deadhead and clear away debris after flowering/Can become invasive; mildew; slugs; snails; leaf and bud eelworms
Good for	Cutting, bees
Looks good with	*Allium*, *Verbena bonariensis*, *Aster*
Selected varieties/cvs	*Anemone* x *hybrida* 'Honorine Jobert'* – white; *A.* x *hybrida* 'September Charm'* – pink; *A. hupehensis* 'Superba' – pale purple-pink

There are more than a hundred different species of *Anemone*, ranging from spring-flowering wood anemones to the tall, border autumn-flowering anemones, often called Japanese anemones. It is the latter that we are concerned with here, and in particular the most popular species, *A.* x *hybrida* and *A. hupehensis*.

These plants are really useful to have in the garden not least because of their late flowering habit. The downside is that once they are established they can become a little invasive, spreading by means of suckering roots: if you don't want an anemone plantation be vigilant, and dig up the offspring as soon as you see them.

The three varieties listed above are all single-flowered, but if you want something with a bit more razzmatazz in the border to liven up (some would say 'clash with') the oranges, yellows and rusts of many other autumn flowering perennials, there are some vivid double forms available, such as the deep pink *A. hupehensis* var. *japonica* 'Pamina'. If you want to play it safe, however, opt for a white variety (the best is *A.* x *hybrida* 'Honorine Jobert'), which will go with anything!

Anthemis tinctoria 'Wargrave'

Anthemis 'Tinpenny Sparkle'

Anthemis

(*an*-them-iss) (Common name – Dyer's chamomile) (Family – Asteraceae)

Type of plant	Hardy, deciduous
Height/Spread	Up to 80cm/60cm
Flowers/Foliage	Daisy-like flowers in white or yellow in summer to autumn/Narrow, feathery, mid-green leaves
Best growing conditions	Sun; light, free-draining soil
Longevity	Approximately 3 years
Propagation	Division, spring; softwood cuttings, early summer
Maintenance/Problems	Taller varieties may need staking; deadhead and cut back after flowering/Mildew; slugs; snails; aphids
Good for	Cutting, bees, dye plant
Looks good with	*Digitalis grandiflora, Verbascum, Delphinium, Campanula*
Selected varieties/cvs	*Anthemis tinctoria* 'E.C. Buxton' – lemon yellow; *A. tinctoria* 'Kelwayi' – bright yellow; *A. tinctoria* 'Sauce Hollandaise' – pale yellow ageing to creamy white; *A. tinctoria* 'Wargrave' – light yellow; *A.* 'Tinpenny Sparkle' – white

The species name of *tinctoria* (from the Latin *tingere* – to colour) and the common name of dyer's chamomile, is indisputable evidence that this plant was, and still is, used as a dye plant. More usually, though, it is popular as a decorative plant, its daisy-like flowers contrasting well with other flowers in the same part of the colour spectrum, as well as blues and purples.

There are a number of species of *Anthemis* but the ones that find their way into garden centres and nurseries, and are therefore more commonly grown, are cultivars of *A. tinctoria*, or are hybrids, usually *A. sancti-johannis*. Perhaps the most widely available is *A. tinctoria* 'E.C. Buxton', which is lemon yellow and ideal for cutting.

Anthemis can be a little tricky to grow if you have anything but well-drained soil. Although they will flower in heavier conditions they will sulk and only last a couple of years at best – take some softwood cuttings as a back-up in case your plant fails.

Aquilegia vulgaris

Aquilegia 'Clementine Rose'

Aquilegia 'Clementine Blue'

Aquilegia 'Clementine White'

Aquilegia

(ak-wil-*ee*-jee-a) (Common name – Columbine, Granny's bonnet) (Family – Ranunculaceae)

Type of plant	Hardy, deciduous
Height/Spread	Up to 90cm/45cm
Flowers/Foliage	Bonnets of spurred flowers, ranging from white and pale lemon to pinks and dark purple, in early summer/Lobed, basal, mid-green leaves
Best growing conditions	Sun, partial shade; all but heavy soil
Longevity	Approximately 3 years
Propagation	Ripe seed, summer; division after flowering – but rarely that successful
Maintenance/Problems	Cut back after flowering unless you want to collect seed/Aphids; sawfly; leaf miner
Good for	Cottage gardens
Looks good with	*Digitalis*, *Cimicifuga*, *Dianthus*, *Campanula*, *Alchemilla*
Selected varieties/cvs	Where do I start? *Aquilegia vulgaris* – violet blue; *A. vulgaris* 'Nivea' – white; *A. vulgaris* var. *stellata* 'Ruby Port' – double, deep maroon; *A. vulgaris* var. *stellata* 'Greenapples' – double, pale green; *A. vulgaris* var. *stellata* 'Nora Barlow'* – double, pink tipped with white; *A.* Clementine series – various

Aquilegia are a quintessential cottage garden plant, together with lavender, *Geranium* and *Alchemilla*, as well as the other suggestions above. They look equally at home in a more modern setting, however; I remember seeing a swathe of low, bronze *Carex* grass through which white and varying shades of purple *Aquilegia* were growing – it looked stunning.

One of the biggest problems with *Aquilegia* is that they are so promiscuous: they will hybridize and set seed freely, creating new offspring that often bear little or no resemblance to the last generation. This is fine if you have a large area that you don't mind them colonizing but it can be frustrating if you want seedlings true to type. I have even noticed plants at garden centres that purport to be a particular variety but look nothing like the description. To make absolutely sure, wait until the plants are in flower before you buy – that way you know exactly what you are getting.

Artemisia canescens

Artemisia

(ar-tem-*ee*-see-a) (Common name – Wormwood) (Family – Asteraceae)

Type of plant	Hardy, deciduous or semi-evergreen, depending on species
Height/Spread	50cm/45cm
Flowers/Foliage	Insignificant – it is rarely grown for its flowers/Intricately lobed, grey or dark green flushed purple leaves, depending on species
Best growing conditions	Sun; well-drained soil
Longevity	Approximately 3 years
Propagation	Softwood cuttings, early summer; division, spring or autumn
Maintenance/Problems	Cut off flower stems unless you specifically want them to flower/Summer humidity can cause mildew
Good for	Foliage colour and contrast
Looks good with	Almost anything!
Selected varieties/cvs	Grey leaves: *Artemisia absinthum* 'Lambrook Mist'*; *A. ludoviciana* 'Valerie Finnis'*; *A.* 'Powis Castle'*; *A. canescens*
	Green leaves: *A. lactiflora* Guizhou Group

The grey-leaved *Artemisia* are primarily foliage plants; their leaves complement just about every other plant in the garden. I think they look particularly good with pink and purple flowers but I have yet to find a combination that doesn't work. Although you will often find it in the perennial display in garden centres, *A.* 'Powis Castle' is actually an evergreen shrub. Its year-long colour makes it very useful as a foil for spring flowering bulbs, especially the dark *Tulipa* 'Negrita' or *T.* 'Queen of the Night'.

The odd group out is the Guizhou Group, which has green leaves, flushed with purple or mahogany, and more attractive white or pink flowers during the summer. They also grow much taller than other species, sometimes reaching up to 1.5m.

Artemisia absinthum is the plant from which the notorious, and once banned, alcoholic drink absinthe is produced, while another species, the herb *Artemisia drancunculus* (tarragon), is highly prized in the kitchen.

Aster divaricatus

Aster x frikartii 'Mönch'

Aster

(*ass*-ter) (Common name – Michaelmas daisy) (Family – Asteraceae)

Type of plant	Hardy, deciduous
Height/Spread	Up to 1m/50cm
Flowers/Foliage	Flat-topped head of daisy flowers in white and shades of pink and purple in autumn/Narrow, mostly lance-shaped, green or grey-green leaves
Best growing conditions	Sun (but see below); moisture retentive soil
Longevity	Approximately 3 years
Propagation	Division, spring or after flowering
Maintenance/Problems	Cut down after flowering and apply mulch/Mildew in *Aster novi-belgii* cultivars
Good for	Cutting, bees
Looks good with	*Echinacea*, *Rudbeckia*, *Crocosmia*
Selected varieties/cvs	*Aster* x *frikartii* 'Mönch'* – purple; *A. novae-angliae* 'Andenken an Alma Pötschke' – salmon pink; *A. novae-angliae* 'Harrington's Pink'* – clear pink; *A. divaricatus* – white

The common name is indicative of the time of year that this group of plants flower: Michaelmas is celebrated on 29 September. They are some of the best autumn-flowering perennials, although many gardeners avoid them because of their susceptibility to mildew. It is true that some older varieties, particularly the *A. novi-belgii* cultivars, suffer from this affliction, but newer ones appear to be less vulnerable.

In my opinion, one of the best varieties by far is *Aster* x *frikartii* 'Mönch'. It has masses of lavender-blue flowers with orange centres held above dark green leaves, and is pretty well trouble-free. It looks good with just about anything you plant alongside it, too. There are some attractive varieties with paler flowers, but I think they look a little washed-out in the fading autumn light, especially if they are planted next to the stronger hues characteristic of many autumn-flowering plants.

Although the vast majority of *Aster* thrive in sunny positions, there is an exception to the rule. *A. divaricatus*, which boasts small white flowers with brownish-yellow centres, is quite happy in a shady spot and brings a welcome addition to the usual ferns, hostas, and other shade-loving plants.

Astilbe 'Amethyst'

Astilbe japonica 'Europa'

Astilbe

(ass-*til*-bee) (Common name – none) (Family – Saxifragaceae)

Type of plant	Hardy, deciduous
Height/Spread	Up to 1m/50cm
Flowers/Foliage	Foamy sprays of flowers in white and shades of pink and purple in summer and early autumn/Dissected green leaves
Best growing conditions	Shade; moisture retentive soil
Longevity	Approximately 4 years
Propagation	Division, autumn
Maintenance/Problems	Cut down in late autumn/Vine weevil
Good for	Cutting, shady areas
Looks good with	*Hosta*, *Ligularia*, Ferns
Selected varieties/cvs	*Astilbe* x *arendsii* 'Fanal' – red; *A.* 'Deutschland' – creamy white; *A.* 'Sprite'* – shell pink; *A.* 'Amethyst' – purple; *A. japonica* 'Europa' – white tinged pale purple-pink

Astilbe are one of the few perennial plants that actually thrive in shady and moist conditions, so they are invaluable when it comes to brightening up a dull corner and adding textural contrast to hostas and ferns. Despite some rather scathing comments from a renowned and influential gardener, I think of *Astilbe* as one of the must-have perennials if you have such conditions in your garden.

In terms of popularity, *Astilbe* have quite a short pedigree, having been in cultivation in Europe only for the last 150 years or so. In the latter part of the 19th century and into the early 20th century, a German nurseryman, Georg Arends, showed interest in the hitherto uncelebrated *Astilbe* and started hybridizing and developing new cultivars. Since then many new forms and colours have been introduced; if you're not sure about which to buy, wait until they are in flower and then pick out the ones you like at your local garden centre or nursery.

Astrantia major 'Moulin Rouge'

Astrantia

(ass-*tran*-tee-a) (Common name – Masterwort) (Family – Apiaceae)

Type of plant	Hardy, deciduous
Height/Spread	Up to 90cm/45cm
Flowers/Foliage	Umbels (surrounded by bracts) of tiny white, pink or blood-red flowers in summer to autumn/Lobed, basal green leaves
Best growing conditions	Sun or part shade; moisture retentive soil
Longevity	Approximately 3 years
Propagation	Division, spring
Maintenance/Problems	Deadhead regularly/Usually trouble-free
Good for	Cutting, bees
Looks good with	Almost anything!
Selected varieties/cvs	*Astrantia major* subsp. *involucrata* 'Shaggy'* – white with green-tipped bracts; *A.* 'Buckland' – soft pink; *A.* 'Hadspen Blood' – reddish purple; *A. major* 'Moulin Rouge' – red-purple; *A. major* 'Venice' – dark pink

Astrantia have long been one of the unsung heroes of the perennial border, their pale umbels of delicate individual flowers setting off the more flamboyant border divas. Until, that is, the arrival of the dark, blood-red variety introduced by Nori and Sandra Pope in the late 1980s: *A.* 'Hadspen Blood', which set the trend in the development of new, outstanding varieties. Now, rather than being a 'bit part' player, *Astrantia* are taking centre stage.

If you still favour a paler bloom, then by far the best is *A. major* subsp. *involucrata* 'Shaggy'. You may also find it listed as *A.* 'Margery Fish' – named after the gardener at East Lambrook Manor in Somerset.

Astrantia rarely come true from seed, which causes problems with propagation. If you see a particular variety on sale at a garden centre that does not have the intensity of colour that it should, it is probably because it has been raised from seed. The only way to continue the pure strain of your named *Astrantia* is by division.

Having said that they look good with almost anything, I particularly like them with border *Campanula* or *Salvia* – the contrast in form and texture is good on the eye.

Bergenia 'Autumn Magic'

Bergenia

(bur-*geen*-ee-a) (Common name – Elephant's ears) (Family – Saxifragaceae)

Type of plant	Hardy, usually evergreen
Height/Spread	50cm/40cm
Flowers/Foliage	Bell-shaped flowers on branched sprays in white, through pink to magenta in spring/Broad, rounded, shiny green leaves
Best growing conditions	Will grow anywhere, but avoid bone-dry or waterlogged soil
Longevity	Approximately 3 years
Propagation	Division after flowering; also see below
Maintenance/Problems	Remove dead leaves regularly/Early flowers may be damaged by frost; slugs; snails; vine weevil
Good for	Shady areas
Looks good with	*Pulmonaria*, *Vinca minor*, spring flowering bulbs
Selected varieties/cvs	*Bergenia* 'Abendglut' – deep magenta; *B.* 'Silberlicht'* – white; *B.* 'Schneekönigin' – pale pink; *B.* 'Autumn Magic' – candy pink

I don't think *Bergenia* get the recognition they deserve. They haven't had the sort of 'celebrity' exposure that many perennials, like *Agapanthus* and *Echinacea*, have enjoyed, but they are one of the most useful plants to have in the garden: they will grow just about anywhere, the majority are evergreen (many turning red over winter), and their flowers are open, bright-eyed and bushy-tailed, well before the majority of other perennials have even yawned or poked a shoot through their duvet of protective winter mulch. They are pretty well bomb-proof, and although the flowers don't last that long, the leaves provide a foil for other plants throughout the rest of the year. So next time you are at the garden centre, spare a thought for *Bergenia*!

Bergenia plants do not come true from seed, so the best way to propagate them is by division, or by cutting a section from a root rhizome which has one or more leaf rosettes on it. This is best done straight after flowering or in the autumn. Pop it in a pot with some compost and grow it on a little before planting it in the garden.

What is more, after a few years the centre of the plant may become open, exposing the bare rhizomes. Now is the time to dig it up, divide it, and replant – and get lots more plants for free.

Brunnera macrophylla 'Betty Bowring'

Brunnera

(*brunn*-ur-a) (Common name – none) (Family – Boraginaceae)

Type of plant	Hardy, deciduous
Height/Spread	45cm/60cm
Flowers/Foliage	Sprays of blue or white, forget-me-not-like flowers in spring/Broad, heart-shaped hairy green or variegated leaves
Best growing conditions	Shade; moisture retentive soil
Longevity	Approximately 3 years
Propagation	Division after flowering
Maintenance/Problems	Deadhead; clear away foliage in autumn; cover crowns with grit to minimize slug damage as leaves appear/Slugs; otherwise trouble-free
Good for	Shady areas
Looks good with	*Euphorbia*, *Dicentra*, *Bergenia*, *Geranium*
Selected varieties/cvs	*Brunnera macrophylla* 'Jack Frost'* – silvery leaves with green veins; *B. macrophylla* 'Betty Bowring' – white flowers

Brunnera is one of those perennials that quietly gets on with what it's supposed to do without making a song and dance about it. And that is to provide extensive and interesting ground cover in shady areas during the growing season. Many varieties have variegated foliage; those with cream or silvery variegation brighten even the dullest corner. But there's more – in spring, clouds of frothy blue or white flowers (depending on the variety) appear and seem to hover above the foliage. If you're lucky you may get a second flush of flowers later in the season, but this is not guaranteed.

Campanula lactiflora 'Loddon Anna'

Campanula glomerata 'Superba'

Campanula lactiflora 'Prichard's Variety'

Campanula

(kam-*pan*-u-la) (Common name – Bellflower) (Family – Campanulaceae)

Type of plant	Hardy, deciduous
Height/Spread	Up to 1.2m/60cm (see below)
Flowers/Foliage	Stems of bell-shaped blue, violet, pink or white flowers in summer, early autumn/Toothed, oval, green leaves
Best growing conditions	Sun; fertile, well-drained soil
Longevity	Approximately 3 years
Propagation	Division, spring or autumn; basal cuttings, early summer
Maintenance/Problems	Deadhead regularly; clear away spent foliage in autumn; some taller varieties may need staking/Slugs; snails; rust
Good for	Cutting, bees
Looks good with	*Anthemis*, *Leucanthemum*, *Geranium*, *Verbascum*
Selected varieties/cvs	*Campanula glomerata* 'Superba'* – deep violet purple; *C. lactiflora* 'Loddon Anna'*– pale lilac pink; *C. lactiflora* 'Prichard's Variety'* – violet purple; *C. latifolia* 'Brantwood' – deep violet blue; *C. takesimana* 'Elizabeth' – pale pink

There are so many species and varieties of *Campanula*, ranging from tiny alpines to majestic, back-of-the-border specimens, that it would take a separate book to do them all justice. So I have concentrated on here what we think of as typical border plants, which accounts for the particular dimensions stated above and the range of selected varieties. These are examples of the plants that are most often grown, and are widely available in garden centres and nurseries.

If your plants appear weak or are growing poorly, they may be suffering from rust. This is a fungal disease which manifests itself as small orange pustules on the leaves. Although chemical remedies are available, it is best to catch the disease early. Be vigilant and remove any affected leaves before the disease has a chance to spread; if possible, burn the foliage – on no account compost it. In addition, do not over-feed your plants with nitrogen-based fertilizers: this results in soft growth that can be easily infected.

Campanula look good with many other perennials, but I especially like the contrast in form and colour that members of the 'daisy' family offer – *Anthemis tinctoria* 'Kelwayi' with its sunny yellow flowers looks particularly lovely against the violet-purple flowers of *Campanula lactiflora* 'Prichard's Variety'.

Centaurea dealbata

Centaurea montana 'Alba'

Centaurea montana

Centaurea

(sen-*tor*-ree-a) (Common name – Knapweed) (Family – Asteraceae)

Type of plant	Hardy, deciduous
Height/Spread	60–90cm/30cm
Flowers/Foliage	Soft, thistle-like blue, mauve-pink or white flowers in summer/Lobed, lance-shaped, green leaves
Best growing conditions	Sun; free-draining, verging on poor soil
Longevity	Approximately 4 years
Propagation	Division, spring or autumn; basal cuttings, early summer; seed (see below)
Maintenance/Problems	Deadhead regularly; leave late seedheads over winter; cut back in early spring; may need staking to prevent flopping/Aphids; mildew
Good for	Cutting, bees, 'wild' garden
Looks good with	*Lupinus*, *Geranium*, *Crocosmia*
Selected varieties/cvs	*Centaurea dealbata* – mauve-pink; *C. montana* – blue; *C. montana* 'Alba' – white; *C. montana* 'Parham' – lavender blue; *C. scabiosa* – reddish purple

A challenge for many gardeners is the so-called 'June gap' (although this may not always be in June – it is entirely dependent on the weather), when spring flowers have long since gone, but the main flush of summer flowers hasn't arrived yet. This is when the species *Centaurea montana* and its cultivars can be a very useful addition to the border, especially for nectar-loving insects. If you cut back after flowering you may get another flush of flowers later in the season. They can be a little invasive but not excessively so.

Found in the wild, *C. scabiosa* also makes a garden-worthy plant. Unlike other perennial *Centaurea*, this is best raised from seed, like its cousin, the annual blue cornflower.

Centranthus ruber

Centranthus

(sen-*tran*-thus) (Common name – Valerian) (Family – Valerianaceae)

Type of plant	Hardy, deciduous
Height/Spread	90cm/50cm
Flowers/Foliage	Heads of small, star-shaped red, pink or white flowers in early summer to autumn/Fleshy, lance-shaped, blue-green leaves
Best growing conditions	Sun; free-draining, verging on poor soil
Longevity	Approximately 3 years
Propagation	Division, spring or autumn; seed, spring or autumn
Maintenance/Problems	Deadhead regularly; cut back in autumn/Usually trouble-free
Good for	Cutting, bees, 'wild' garden
Looks good with	*Salvia, Hemerocallis*
Selected varieties/cvs	*Centranthus ruber* – red; *C. ruber* 'Albus' – white with a pink tinge; *C. ruber* 'Snowcloud' – pure white

This perennial has a somewhat loose habit and it naturalizes very easily; both of these factors make it unpopular with some gardeners. I rather like it, however – its long flowering season and relative lack of maintenance make up for the bad points. Add the fact that bees and other pollinating insects like it and you have a plant that makes it into my top 100!

Of the few named cultivars that are available, I particularly like *C. ruber* 'Albus'. You can hardly call it the star of the show, but its airy clusters of white flowers tinged with pink show off almost every other plant in the border, especially those with prominent, colourful blooms like *Hemerocallis*. You will often find plants popping up that bear no resemblance to their parent – the pink one pictured is an example of this – keep it if you like it but otherwise weed it out.

Although the common name of *Centranthus* is valerian, it should not be confused with another plant with the same common name: *Valeriana officinalis*, which is a completely different plant. This is a good example of where knowing the Latin name avoids confusion.

Chrysanthemum 'Gala Burgundy'

Chrysanthemum

(kriss-*an*-the-mum) (Common name – none) (Family – Asteraceae)

Type of plant	Hardy, deciduous
Height/Spread	70cm/50cm
Flowers/Foliage	Daisy-like flowers in many colours, from white through yellow and orange to pink and red in autumn/Alternate, lobed green leaves
Best growing conditions	Sun; moderately fertile, free-draining, soil
Longevity	Approximately 3 years
Propagation	Division, spring; basal cuttings, spring
Maintenance/Problems	Cut back after flowering and mulch in very cold areas; taller varieties may need support/Rust
Good for	Cutting
Looks good with	Almost any other late-flowering perennial
Selected varieties/cvs	*Chrysanthemum* 'Clara Curtis' – single, pink; *C.* 'Mary Stoker' – single, apricot yellow; *C.* 'Mrs Jessie Cooper' – single, deep pink; *C.* 'Nantyderry Sunshine'* – yellow, semi-pompom; *C.* 'Ruby Mound'* – double, maroon red; *C.* Gala Series – various
☠ BEWARE ☠	Can cause skin irritation

The first thing to say is that here we are dealing with the hardy, perennial border *Chrysanthemum*. Florist or exhibition varieties are unlikely to stand up to the vagaries of winter weather so they are not included.

It seems to me that *Chrysanthemum* are often overlooked nowadays when it comes to recommendations for autumn-flowering perennials. This may be because they have an undeserved reputation for being a bit fuddy-duddy, or because the 'must-have' horticultural spotlight has fallen on 'prairie plants' (such as *Helenium* and *Echinacea*), many of which flower long into the autumn. Either way, spare a thought for this stalwart of the traditional border when you are next choosing autumn-flowering plants.

I tend to prefer the single-flowered varieties, mainly because they are better for pollinating insects such as bees, but a number of the semi-double and double varieties are worth making room for, such as one of the Gala Series.

Cirsium rivulare 'Atropurpureum'

Cirsium

(*sir*-see-um) (Common name – Thistle) (Family – Asteraceae)

Type of plant	Hardy, deciduous
Height/Spread	Up to 1.5m/50cm
Flowers/Foliage	Thistle-like flowers in pink or rosy purple in summer/Lobed, spiny green or green-grey leaves
Best growing conditions	Sun; moderately fertile, moisture retentive soil
Longevity	Approximately 3 years
Propagation	Division, spring; seed, spring (see below)
Maintenance/Problems	Cut back after flowering to prevent invasive seeding/Mildew
Good for	Cutting, bees
Looks good with	*Papaver*, *Astrantia*, *Salvia*, grasses
Selected varieties/cvs	*Cirsium rivulare* 'Atropurpureum' – rosy purple; *C. japonicum* 'Pink Beauty' – soft pink

When I asked my friend who owns a plant nursery which plant surprises her the most in terms of popularity, it was this one – and more particularly *Cirsium rivulare* 'Atropurpureum'. As this is a bit of a mouthful, many people ask for the 'maroony-coloured thistle', and she knows exactly what they mean! I have a feeling that its current fame can be traced back fairly recently, to the Chelsea Flower Show of 2000 when Arne Maynard and Piet Oudolf used it extensively in their award-winning garden – and stunning it looked, too, intermingled with *Salvia* and *Astrantia*.

The other main species is *C. japonicum*, which has a number of cultivars including 'Pink Beauty' and 'Rose Beauty'. Both of these are widely available as seed.

Cirsium is one of those perennials that complement so many others without drawing attention to itself. Its reticence to jump out at you makes it ideal in a supporting role, in much the same way as *Verbena bonariensis*.

One final reflection: who would have thought that so many people would actually want to plant a thistle in their garden…!

Clematis integrifolia

Clematis

(*klem*-a-tis) (Common name – none) (Family – Ranunculaceae)

Type of plant	Hardy, deciduous
Height/Spread	Up to 1.5m/75cm
Flowers/Foliage	Nodding, bell or saucer-shaped white, pink or purple flowers in summer/Pairs of oval or lance-shaped green leaves
Best growing conditions	Sun; well-drained, humus rich soil
Longevity	Approximately 4 years
Propagation	Division, spring; softwood cuttings, spring
Maintenance/Problems	Cut back to almost ground level in autumn/Slugs; whitefly; scale insects
Good for	Ground cover or as low climber
Looks good with	*Rosa*, *Delphinium*, *Allium*
Selected varieties/cvs	*Clematis heracleifolia* 'Roundway Blue Bird' – fragrant, dark blue; *C. integrifolia* – purple-blue; *C. integrifolia* 'Alba' white; *C.* 'Petit Faucon'* – deep blue-purple; *C.* 'Savannah' – dark pink

Ask someone to describe a clematis and they will undoubtedly refer to the climbing plant. There is, however, a whole raft of herbaceous clematis that make excellent specimens for the perennial border. It is true that the majority will require some sort of support in the form of hazel twigs, or perhaps another plant, such as a rose, through which to grow, but they can also be left to sprawl and find their own way along the border.

I saw a lovely rose/clematis combination in a garden near to where my daughter lives in Hertfordshire: *Clematis* 'Petit Faucon' – a deep blue-purple – had been allowed to scramble through *Rosa* 'Graham Thomas' – a fully double, rich yellow English rose. The juxtaposition of the single and double flower forms and the complementary colours was an inspired piece of planting. I have also seen a pink-flowered *Clematis* (unfortunately I wasn't able to discover which one it was) that had been left to edge its way across and through *Bergenia* after it had finished flowering. This combination worked very well too, the pink *Clematis* flowers 'replacing' the spent, pink blooms of the *Bergenia*.

Convallaria majalis

Convallaria

(kon-val-*lair*-ree-a) (Common name – Lily of the valley) (Family – Convallariaceae)

Type of plant	Hardy, deciduous
Height/Spread	25cm/30cm
Flowers/Foliage	Fragrant white or pink bell-shaped flowers in late spring and early summer/Broad, lance-shaped green leaves
Best growing conditions	Part shade or shade; moist, slightly alkaline, humus rich soil
Longevity	Approximately 4 years
Propagation	Division, spring after flowering, or autumn
Maintenance/Problems	Do not allow soil to dry out; deadhead; mulch in autumn/Grey mould
Good for	Ground cover in damp shade
Looks good with	*Polygonatum*, *Corydalis*. Plant a shade-loving *Geranium* between to provide interest when the *Convallaria* have died back
Selected varieties/cvs	*Convallaria majalis** – white; *C. majalis* var. *rosea* – pink; *C. majalis* 'Hardwick Hall' – large white flowers; *C. majalis* 'Albostriata' – striped, creamy-white variegated leaves
☠ **BEWARE** ☠	All parts of the plant are toxic

A moist, shady spot in the garden is often one of those places that leave people scratching their head as to what to plant there. Scratch no more! This well-beloved spring flowering perennial fits the bill perfectly. You can buy potted plants at your local garden centre or nursery; alternatively, scrounge some from a neighbour. Don't allow the rhizomatous roots to dry out, though; the dry ones that are often for sale in plastic bags at supermarkets and garden centres will languish rather than flourish, and it may be some time before you see any return for your money.

My favourite is the straightforward *C. majalis* with its tiny white, highly fragrant bells – for something a little more unusual go for the pink-flowered one; or if you are looking for size, then *C. majalis* 'Hardwick Hall', with its slightly larger flowers, is the one for you.

One of the delights of spring – other than welcoming back swallows and house martins – is picking a bunch of lily of the valley to set on the breakfast table; my muesli seems to taste so much better!

Coreopsis 'Limerock Passion'

Coreopsis 'Sunray'

Coreopsis

(kor-ee-*op*-siss) Common name – Tickseed) (Family – Asteraceae)

Type of plant	Hardy, deciduous
Height/Spread	50cm/45cm
Flowers/Foliage	Daisy-like flowers in yellow, red, pink or white in summer and early autumn/Narrow, often divided or feathered green leaves
Best growing conditions	Sun; moisture retentive but well-drained soil
Longevity	Approximately 3 years
Propagation	Division, spring; basal cuttings, spring; seed, spring
Maintenance/Problems	Deadhead regularly; cut back hard in autumn after flowering/Mildew
Good for	Cutting, bees, butterflies
Looks good with	*Salvia*, *Verbascum*, *Echinops*, *Achillea*, grasses
Selected varieties/cvs	*Coreopsis verticillata* 'Moonbeam'* – pale yellow; *C.* 'Limerock Ruby' – ruby red; *C. 'Limerock* Passion' – dark pink; *C.* 'Sunray' – yellow; *C.* 'Tequila Sunrise' – yellow with red

Coreopsis are not the longest lived of perennials – indeed, some begin to look a little worse for wear after only a couple of years. Divide and replace them regularly and you will have a superb display for years. Many *Coreopsis* are prolific self-seeders, but often their progeny are a little lack-lustre compared with the parents, so vegetative propagation is the best way to keep a true strain.

The majority of *Coreopsis* flowers are yellow with slight variations. Of the recent newer varieties, however, the one that caused many a gardener's heart to flutter was *C.* 'Limerock Ruby', with its ruby red flower and darker foliage. This was introduced by Limerock Plant Farm in Rhode Island in 2001, and since then other red and dark pink forms have emerged, such as *C.* 'Limerock Passion' (pictured), and *C.* 'Limerock Ruby' takes some beating.

Coreopsis have become popular owing in part to the style of planting known as 'prairie': *Coreopsis* lend themselves to being planted in waves, one of the 'prairie' characteristics. Having said that, they also look grand in a traditional perennial border, so there is no excuse for not planting it!

Corydalis lutea

Corydalis flexuosa 'China Blue'

Corydalis

(kor-ree-*day*-liss) (Common name – none) (Family – Papaveraceae)

Type of plant	Hardy, deciduous
Height/Spread	30cm/20cm
Flowers/Foliage	Spikes of tubular yellow, white, pink, red or blue flowers in spring/Finely dissected, grey-green leaves
Best growing conditions	Partial shade, sun; well-drained, humus rich soil
Longevity	Approximately 3 years
Propagation	Division, autumn
Maintenance/Problems	None/Slugs; snails
Good for	Woodland edge
Looks good with	*Convallaria majalis*
Selected varieties/cvs	*Corydalis flexuosa* 'China Blue' – sky blue; *C. lutea* – yellow; *C. solida* subsp. *solida* 'Beth Evans' – pale pink; *C. solida* subsp. *solida* 'George Baker'* – brick red; *C.* 'Tory MP' – blue

It's very easy to forget where you have planted *Corydalis* because both flowers and foliage of the majority of plants die back over the summer; the leaves reappear in autumn. It's worth marking the spot with a few twigs so you don't inadvertently dig it up if you decide to plant something new in the area.

If you are thinking of choosing a *Corydalis* to plant in your garden, set aside your political persuasions for a moment and consider *C.* 'Tory MP'. It has lovely large, dark blue, fragrant flowers; as well as flowering in the spring, it's an exception to the rule and often has a second flush in the autumn.

Corydalis flowers aren't restricted to blue; you can get white, pink and red, but I particularly like the yellow of *C. lutea* (the Latin species name is the give-away – *lutea* means golden yellow). It sings out from a shady spot whereas the blue-flowered varieties tend to all but disappear.

Crocosmia masoniorum

Crocosmia

(kro-*koss*-mee-a) (Common name – Montbretia) (Family – Iridaceae)

Type of plant	Hardy, deciduous
Height/Spread	Up to 70cm/35cm
Flowers/Foliage	Stems of star or funnel-shaped yellow, orange or red flowers in summer and early autumn/Narrow, sword-shaped, green leaves
Best growing conditions	Sun; any soil, except very dry
Longevity	Approximately 3 years
Propagation	Division, early spring
Maintenance/Problems	Mulch in autumn/Red spider mite in hot, dry summers
Good for	Cutting
Looks good with	*Achillea, Dahlia, Helenium, Rudbeckia, Foeniculum*
Selected varieties/cvs	*Crocosmia* 'Lucifer'* – deep red; *C.* 'Spitfire' – orange; *C.* x *crocosmiiflora* 'Star of the East'* – golden orange; *C.* x *crocosmiiflora* 'Morning Light' – clear yellow; *C. masoniorum* – orange

Often when you mention *Crocosmia* (or its common name, montbretia) a groan goes round the room. 'Won't have it in my garden.' 'That old weed – you must be joking.' It's true that the ubiquitous *Crocosmia* x *crocosmiiflora,* first created in 1879, can become a nuisance in gardens (and beyond) because of its vigour, but there are many named varieties that are well worth growing. I favour the clear yellow flowers of *C.* x *crocosmiiflora* 'Morning Light', or the fiery orange of *C.* x *crocosmiiflora* 'Spitfire', and you can't go far wrong with *C.* 'Lucifer' if you want a rich red.

All *Crocosmia* contrast well with other autumn flowering perennials, especially those of the daisy family, such as *Dahlia*, *Helenium* and *Rudbeckia.* I also like to grow it alongside *Foeniculum vulgare* 'Purpureum' with its feathery bronze foliage.

Dahlia 'Bishop of Llandaff'

Dahlia 'Inns Gerrie Hoek'

Dahlia 'Moonfire'

Dahlia

(*day*-lee-a) (Common name – none) (Family – Asteraceae)

Type of plant	Tender, deciduous
Height/Spread	Up to 1m/45cm
Flowers/Foliage	Open or double, daisy-like white, pink, yellow, orange or red flowers in autumn/Pairs of deeply cut or divided green leaves
Best growing conditions	Sun; well-drained, fertile soil
Longevity	Approximately 3 years
Propagation	Division of tubers, early spring; basal cuttings, spring
Maintenance/Problems	Lift tubers in autumn (see below)/Snails; earwigs
Good for	Cutting, single varieties are good for bees
Looks good with	*Helenium*, *Rudbeckia*, *Foeniculum*
Selected varieties/cvs	*Dahlia* 'Dark Desire' – single, chocolatey red; *D.* 'Summer Night' – cactus, dark maroon; *D.* 'Honka'* – spidery, pale yellow; *D.* 'Magenta Star'* – single, purple-pink; *D.* 'Inns Gerrie Hoek' – pink-purple with white edge; *D.* 'Bishop of Llandaff' – red; *D.* 'Moonfire' – orange and yellow

When I ask people whether or not they grow dahlias, the reply always seems to be, 'No, but my granddad did.' Are dahlias 'ageist'? Do you have to be of a certain age – and gender – before you are allowed to grow them? I hope not; and in fact I think that dahlias have been undergoing a bit of a renaissance. I'm pleased to say that this applies especially to the single-flowered varieties, which seem to blend in with other plants so much more readily than the more flamboyant double varieties, adding extra colour and form to the late-summer and autumn border. They also make excellent cut flowers. There are so many to choose from, but one of the most well-known varieties is *D.* 'Bishop of Llandaff'. If you are looking for a variety that is particularly attractive to bees then look no further than *D.* 'Moonfire'.

Dahlias are tender, and need a little more care and attention than hardy perennials. Wait until all risk of frost has passed before planting out cutting-raised plants or dry tubers. When the first frost of the autumn blackens the foliage, lift the tubers, dry them off, then pack them in bone-dry compost in a frost-free place over winter.

Delphinium 'Foxhill Nina'

Delphinium 'Michael Ayres'

Delphinium

(del-*fin*-ee-um) (Common name – none) (Family – Ranunculaceae)

Type of plant	Hardy, deciduous
Height/Spread	Up to 1.5m/75cm
Flowers/Foliage	Tall spikes of mainly white, pink or blue shades in summer/Green leaves with 3 or 5 lobes, arranged spirally around stem
Best growing conditions	Sun; fertile, free-draining soil
Longevity	Approximately 3 years
Propagation	Basal cutting, spring; division, spring; seed, spring after period of stratification
Maintenance/Problems	Put supports in place before flower stems get too tall; cut back in autumn/Slugs; snails; powdery mildew; leaf miner; black leaf spot
Good for	Cutting
Looks good with	*Rosa*, *Achillea*, *Hemerocallis*, *Papaver*
Selected varieties/cvs	*Delphinium grandiflorum* 'Blue Butterfly' – blue; *D.* 'Michael Ayres' – purple with blue tip; *D.* 'Guinevere' – lavender pink; *D.* 'Sunkissed'* – very pale yellow; *D.* 'Foxhill Nina'* – pale pink-lilac
☠ **BEWARE** ☠	*Delphinium* are considered to be as good as toxic (see below)

Many people have trouble growing *Delphinium* – me included. It probably has something to do with my less than free-draining soil, and the fact that the slugs appear to be quicker off the mark than I am! I now grow *Aconitum* instead. If I could wave a magic wand, I would love to grow *D.* 'Min', with its purplish-violet flowers, simply because my childhood nickname was Min.

If you are fortunate enough to have 'delphinium digits', as well as green fingers, there is a plethora of stately flower-laden plants just waiting to be grown. In fact there are so many different species, let alone cultivars, to be found throughout the world that by far the best way to decide which ones to grow is to see them in flower at a nursery or garden centre first.

Take care when handling *Delphinium* – the sap may cause skin irritation and all parts of the plant can cause severe discomfort if ingested.

Dianthus carthusianorum

Dianthus 'Romance'

Dianthus 'Cover Story'

Dianthus

(di-*an*-thus) (Common name – Pink) (Family – Caryophyllaceae)

Type of plant	Hardy, evergreen
Height/Spread	40cm/40cm
Flowers/Foliage	Single or double white or pink (or combination of both), often scented flowers with overlapping petals in summer/Long, slender, pointed green or grey-green leaves
Best growing conditions	Sun; fertile, alkaline, free-draining soil
Longevity	Approximately 3 years
Propagation	Cuttings, summer
Maintenance/Problems	Deadhead regularly/Occasionally slugs and aphids
Good for	Cutting, edging
Looks good with	Short bearded *Iris*, *Aquilegia*, *Nigella*
Selected varieties/cvs	*Dianthus* 'Doris'* – double, pink with salmon-pink band; *D.* 'Gran's Favourite'* – double, white; *D.* 'Romance' – double, salmon pink, scented; *D.* 'Cover Story' – magenta and white; *D.* 'Devon Glow'* – semi-double, lavender purple; *D. caryophyllus* – single, deep pink-purple, highly scented; *D. carthusianorum* – single, deep pink

As a child living in Sussex, I remember our garden filled to overflowing with pinks. We had a market garden and plant centre, and I think if my dad had had the time and inclination, we could have held a National Collection of them! I know now that the key to our success in growing them was the chalky, free-draining soil – the one thing above all others that will kill them off is wet feet in the winter. If your soil falls short of providing perfect conditions for them, try growing pinks in containers, where you can tailor-make the optimum mixture, adding grit and a little lime if necessary.

Everyone has their favourites – especially grandmas! I love all forms of *Dianthus*, particularly the old-fashioned ones, and most of all *D. caryophyllus* – the clove pink, used by apothecaries and herbalists. There are lots of lovely new introductions, however, including the 'Devon Series' which contain many outstanding varieties.

Dicentra spectabilis

Dicentra eximia 'Snowdrift'

Dicentra

(di-*sen*-tra) (Common name – Bleeding heart) (Family – Papaveraceae)

Type of plant	Hardy, deciduous
Height/Spread	Up to 1m/50cm
Flowers/Foliage	Dangling, heart-shaped white or pink flowers in late spring and summer/Divided green or glaucous green leaves
Best growing conditions	Part shade; moist, humus rich soil
Longevity	Approximately 3 years
Propagation	Division, early spring or autumn; root cuttings, dormant season
Maintenance/Problems	Cut back after flowering/Slugs; snails
Good for	Woodland area
Looks good with	*Brunnera, Bergenia, Pulmonaria*
Selected varieties/cvs	*Dicentra spectabilis* – rose pink and white; *D. eximia* 'Snowdrift' – white; *D.* 'King of Hearts' – dark pink-red
☠ BEWARE ☠	All parts are mildly toxic; foliage may cause allergic reaction

I have a love–hate relationship with *Dicentra*. I feel I ought to love them but I just can't. I think it must be the common name, bleeding heart, that put me off as a child. If I had been told they were called 'lady in the bath' (if you turn the flower upside down, you will see why), I might be more sympathetic towards them.

I say I feel I ought to love them because they are such a useful plant to have in a shady spot, especially the all-white variety *D. spectabilis* 'Alba', which teams up so well with *Brunnera* and *Pulmonaria.* The compact variety *D.* 'King of Hearts' has more glaucous leaves than many others, which contrast well with its pinky red flowers.

Dicentra is now officially known as *Lamprocapnos* but is still widely known as *Dicentra*.

Dierama pulcherrimum

Dierama

(di-er-*raa*-ma) (Common name – Angel's fishing rods) (Family – Iridaceae)

Type of plant	Hardy, evergreen – but can look tatty by autumn
Height/Spread	Up to 1.2m/50cm
Flowers/Foliage	Dainty, bell-shaped, pendulous, mainly pink or mauve flowers in summer/Grassy tufts of long, narrow, green-grey leaves
Best growing conditions	Full sun; fertile, free-draining soil
Longevity	Approximately 5 years
Propagation	Division, spring
Maintenance/Problems	Remove any dead foliage in spring/Usually trouble-free
Good for	Any planting scheme, cutting
Looks good with	*Iris, Erigeron, Astrantia*
Selected varieties/cvs	*Dierama* 'Guinevere' – white; *D.* 'Lancelot' – shell pink; *D.* 'Merlin' – blackberry purple; *D. pulcherrimum* – variable, pale pink to rich purple

When I first encountered these beautiful plants, many years ago, I couldn't believe that they were hardy, especially as so many people had told me they wouldn't survive a winter. What I found out later was that it isn't the cold *per se* that kills them off but frozen, waterlogged soil.

Bearing the common name of angel's fishing rods, it is tempting to grow them by water, and this is fine as long as the soil isn't too moist. Free-draining soil is the key – that, and not disturbing them too much. Move them and they will sulk. This makes propagation a little tricky, as the only way to guarantee true offspring is by dividing the parent plant.

You can grow *Dierama* from seed, but it is a little hit and miss as to what you will get and you will have to be patient because it will be at least three years before they are ready to flower.

Far better is to buy a named cultivar from the garden centre nursery – some of the most spectacular introductions have been from Jim Cave in Cornwall, with his varieties named after Camelot characters: *D.* 'Merlin', *D.* 'Guinevere' and *D.* 'Lancelot'.

Digitalis grandiflora

Digitalis

(dij-it-*ah*-liss) (Common name – Foxglove) (Family – Scrophulariaceae)

Type of plant	Hardy, evergreen
Height/Spread	80cm/40cm
Flowers/Foliage	Spikes of tubular flowers in summer/Basal rosettes of lance-shaped, green leaves
Best growing conditions	Sun or part shade; any soil
Longevity	Approximately 4 years
Propagation	Seed, spring; basal cuttings, spring
Maintenance/Problems	Deadhead and remove decaying leaves regularly/Usually trouble-free
Good for	Any border situation
Looks good with	*Papaver*, *Rosa*, *Leucanthemum*, *Campanula*, *Polemonium*, *Salvia*
Selected varieties/cvs	*Digitalis grandiflora** – yellow; *D.* x *mertonensis** – strawberry pink; *D.* 'John Innes Tetra' – yellow with honey brown
☠ BEWARE ☠	All parts are toxic

Mention foxglove to most people and they immediately think of the biennial plant, *Digitalis purpurea* with its mauve-pink flowers growing in woodland clearings or colonizing neglected areas. There are many attractive cultivated varieties of this original species but they, too, are biennial. There are, however, a number of perennial foxgloves which are every bit as striking, and because they last for a few years are well worth growing in the border.

I think the one that catches many people unawares is the yellow-flowered *D. grandiflora*. It doesn't grow too tall – about 60 to 80cm – and looks grand with *Polemonium* or *Leucanthemum*. I have also seen it growing with *Rosa* 'Graham Thomas' – the toning yellow hues, and contrast in flower form looked stunning.

Also worth growing is the crushed strawberry pink *D. mertonensis* – you really have to see this colour to believe it. Put it alongside *Papaver* 'Patty's Plum' and you have a veritable fruity concoction, although the two in combination can look a little leaden without something airy like the lacy white flowers of *Allium neapolitanum* Cowanii Group to lift them.

A word of warning: all *Digitalis* are toxic, so be vigilant when handling them.

Doronicum x *excelsum* 'Harpur Crewe'

Doronicum 'Miss Mason'

Doronicum

(dor-*on*-ee-kum) (Common name – Leopard's bane) (Family – Asteraceae)

Type of plant	Hardy, deciduous
Height/Spread	Up to 60cm/40cm
Flowers/Foliage	Daisy-like, yellow flowers in spring/Soft oval or heart-shaped green leaves
Best growing conditions	Dappled shade, but will tolerate sun; fertile, free-draining soil
Longevity	Approximately 4 years
Propagation	Division, spring
Maintenance/Problems	Deadhead and remove decaying leaves regularly/Slugs; snails; powdery mildew
Good for	Shady situations
Looks good with	Spring flowering bulbs, *Pulmonaria*, *Brunnera*
Selected varieties/cvs	*Doronicum* x *excelsum* 'Harpur Crewe' – yellow; *D.* 'Miss Mason' – yellow; *D.* 'Little Leo' – yellow (shorter variety); *D. orientale* 'Magnificum' – yellow

Doronicum is one of the earliest flowering perennials, bringing cheery, daisy-like flowers to the border in spring. Varieties of *Doronicum orientale*, such as 'Magnificum', look lovely with tulips in the cultivated border.

As far as I can tell, all *Doronicum* have yellow flowers, which doesn't mean to say that plant breeders won't at some time produce differently coloured cultivars: there are very few border perennials that haven't come under the spotlight, with the result that new and exciting variations have been introduced.

Its common name of Leopard's bane comes from the fact that it is deadly to animals. In fact John Gerard, writing in his *Herbal* of 1597, affirms that 'it killeth Panthers ... Wolves, and all kinds of wilde beasts, being given them with flesh'. And it 'killeth dogs, it is very certain, and found out by trial'. And yet 'this herbe or the root thereof is not deadly to man' – although I'm not sure I would like to put it to the test, despite what Gerard says!

Echinacea purpurea 'Harvest Moon'

Echinacea purpurea 'Pow Wow'

Echinacea purpurea 'Primadonna White'

Echinacea purpurea

Echinacea

(ek-in-*ay*-see-a) (Common name – Coneflower) (Family – Asteraceae)

Type of plant	Hardy, deciduous
Height/Spread	Up to 60cm/40cm
Flowers/Foliage	Daisy-like, cone-centred, pink-purple or white-cream flowers in summer and autumn/Bristly basal dark green leaves
Best growing conditions	Sun; deep, humus rich, well-drained soil
Longevity	Approximately 4 years
Propagation	Root cuttings, dormant season; seed, spring
Maintenance/Problems	Deadhead and remove decaying leaves regularly/Usually trouble-free
Good for	Cutting, bees, butterflies
Looks good with	*Geranium*, *Verbascum*, *Agastache*, *Verbena*
Selected varieties/cvs	*Echinacea purpurea* – pink-purple; *E. purpurea* 'Pow Wow' – rose pink; *E. purpurea* 'Harvest Moon' – butter yellow; *E. purpurea* 'Primadonna White' – white

Echinacea are sometimes confused with *Rudbeckia*: one reason for this is that they both share the common name of coneflower. In fact, I have even seen them mixed up in a nursery catalogue! The easiest way to tell them apart is to look at, and touch, the centre of the flower. *Echinacea* comes from the Greek *echinos*, which roughly translated means 'spiny'. The centre of *Echinacea* does indeed feel slightly prickly or spiny, whereas the centre of *Rudbeckia* is much softer.

Most people grow the straightforward *Echinacea purpurea* which has, as its name implies, purpley flowers. There are lots of new introductions, though, many of which have kept the same basic colour tone, but others have broken into the white and yellow part of the spectrum.

There is ongoing debate about the efficacy of *Echinacea* as a medicinal herb: some people swear by its ability to reduce the chances of catching a cold and boost the immune system, while others dismiss such claims as nonsense. Either way, all varieties are well worth growing in the garden for their attractiveness alone, particularly if you want to attract beneficial insects into your garden: bees, especially, love *Echinacea*.

Echinops ritro 'Veitch's Blue'

Echinops

(*ek*-in-ops) (Common name – Globe thistle) (Family – Asteraceae)

Type of plant	Hardy, deciduous
Height/Spread	Up to 1.2m/75cm
Flowers/Foliage	Spheres of tiny blue or white flowers in summer/Spiny, lobed green leaves
Best growing conditions	Sun; well-drained soil
Longevity	Approximately 4 years
Propagation	Root cuttings, dormant season; division, spring
Maintenance/Problems	Leave seedheads over winter for birds/Aphids
Good for	Cutting, bees, moths
Looks good with	*Agastache*, *Geranium*, *Verbascum*, *Verbena*
Selected varieties/cvs	*Echinops bannaticus* 'Taplow Blue'* – steel blue; *E. ritro* 'Veitch's Blue' – blue; *E. sphaerocephalus* 'Arctic Glow' – grey-white

While visiting a garden I overheard a lady ask her friend what the blue 'sputnik' flowers were. I couldn't help but think what an apt description that was; *Echinops* really do look like something from outer space – quite different from almost any other flower in the garden. The curiosity factor alone makes them worth growing, but add to that the fact that they are adored by bees and other pollinating insects, and they are good for cutting, then you have a perfect candidate to include in your perennial border.

In addition, *Echinops* can cope with very dry conditions; its branching taproot searches down into the soil for moisture much further than many other perennials. If you are in an area that suffers from droughts and hose-pipe bans, *Echinops* is one plant that will survive in such conditions.

My favourite has to be *Echinops ritro* 'Veitch's Blue': it's a little less unwieldy than some other varieties and the flowers are of the most intense blue. There is a white variety, *E. sphaerocephalus* 'Arctic Glow', although in my view the colour is more grubby white than wash-day white. Nevertheless, instead of being the focus of attention, it has a place as a foil for brighter-coloured perennials.

Epimedium sp.

Epimedium x *versicolor* 'Sulphureum'

Epimedium

(ep-ee-*me*-dee-um) (Common name – Barrenwort) (Family – Berberidaceae)

Type of plant	Hardy, deciduous or evergreen, depending on species
Height/Spread	Up to 45cm/50cm
Flowers/Foliage	Sprays of spidery white, yellow, pink or purple flowers in spring/Wiry stems with divided, oval, lance-shaped or heart-shaped, sometimes mottled, green leaves
Best growing conditions	Shade or part shade; moist, well-drained soil
Longevity	Approximately 4 years
Propagation	Division, autumn
Maintenance/Problems	Cut back old growth in autumn/Aphids; slugs; snails; vine weevil
Good for	Woodland area
Looks good with	*Hosta, Brunnera, Pulmonaria*
Selected varieties/cvs	*Epimedium grandiflorum* 'Lilafee' – violet purple; *E.* x *versicolor* 'Sulphureum'* – yellow; *E.* 'Amber Queen' – apricot bronze

Like many other woodland plants, *Epimedium* can sometimes be overlooked in favour of their brighter, brasher border brethren. But look carefully and you will see delicate flowers above beautiful leaves, providing interest at the beginning of the growing season. These are flowers that call for minute examination – it's worth hunkering down because the more you look, the more you see. For example, some *Epimedium* have spurred flowers that remind me of mini *Aquilegia*; others have subtle toned shading, not always obvious unless you are eye level with them; others have veined, mottled leaves, the lace-like pattern of which demands closer scrutiny.

There are many *Epimedium* to choose from, but I think my favourite has to be *E. grandiflorum* 'Lilafee', with its beautiful, dainty, pale violet-purple flowers – no wonder it is often referred to as 'lilac fairy'.

Eremurus himalaicus

Eremurus

(er-ee-*mu*-russ) (Common name – Foxtail lily) (Family – Asphodelaceae)

Type of plant	Hardy, deciduous
Height/Spread	Up to 2m/50cm
Flowers/Foliage	Usually single spike of dozens of tiny white, pink or yellow flowers in early summer/Tufts of long, strappy, pointed green leaves
Best growing conditions	Full sun; rich, well-drained soil
Longevity	Approximately 5 years
Propagation	Division, summer or early autumn; seed, autumn
Maintenance/Problems	None/Generally trouble-free
Good for	Bees
Looks good with	*Rosa, Euphorbia, Geranium*
Selected varieties/cvs	*Eremurus robustus** – pale pink; *E.* x *isabellinus* 'Cleopatra' – peachy orange; *E.* x *isabellinus* 'Rosalind' – bright pink; *E. stenophyllus** – yellow; *E. himalaicus* – white

If you want to make a really bold statement in your garden you can probably do no better than to plant some *Eremurus*. Although they flower for only a relatively short time, they certainly provide a 'wow' factor when they do. Some will grow up to 2 metres and more, their upright, foxbrush-like spikes towering over many other specimens in the border. Dot one or two through the planting space and they will look like gangly teenagers, not quite happy with their own company – but group several together and you will get a throng of graceful spires, each reflecting the others' elegance.

Eremurus can be tricky if they have anything less than good drainage, especially during the winter. The fleshy, finger-like roots will rot if they are surrounded by soil that holds too much moisture. The best way to alleviate this problem is to perch the crown and roots on a dome of horticultural grit and then backfill. The crown needs to be above the surface of the soil and should never be covered.

If you plant *Eremurus robustus* and it is happy with its lot, it will begin to self-seed; other species are best propagated by carefully dividing the plants after flowering.

Erigeron 'Sommerabend'

Erigeron glaucus 'Wayne Roderick'

Erigeron

(er-*ig*-er-on) (Common name – Fleabane) (Family – Asteraceae)

Type of plant	Hardy, deciduous
Height/Spread	Up to 60cm/45cm
Flowers/Foliage	Daisy-like flowers in various colours with yellow eye in summer/Usually basal, toothed green leaves
Best growing conditions	Sun; moderately fertile, free-draining soil
Longevity	Approximately 4 years
Propagation	Division, spring; softwood or basal cuttings, spring
Maintenance/Problems	Deadhead; clear away debris in autumn/Powdery mildew
Good for	Coastal conditions, bees
Looks good with	*Knautia*, *Lavandula*, *Verbena*
Selected varieties/cvs	*Erigeron karvinskianus** – white turning to reddish purple; *E. glaucus* 'Sea Breeze' – lavender pink; *E. glaucus* 'Wayne Roderick' – lavender; *E.* 'Dunkelste Aller'* – violet blue; *E.* 'Sommerabend'– violet blue

In many ways *Erigeron* are early versions of Michaelmas daisies – they have similar daisy-like flowers with yellow centres and they are also good for pollinating insects. Given the popularity of Michaelmas daisies, I am surprised that *Erigeron* are not more widely grown. Perhaps it has something to do with its common name, fleabane – let's face it, this has a less than attractive ring to it. However, as the name implies, it is valuable for repelling fleas and other unwanted insects – a virtue that is not in such great demand these days but proved very useful before the advent of insecticides. During the summer months I often place a vase of *Erigeron* and *Tanacetum vulgare* (tansy – also an insect repellent) in the kitchen and find that flies are less troublesome.

Many varieties of *Erigeron* have been bred in Germany and therefore bear German names: *E.* 'Sommerneuschnee' means 'new snow in summer', a white variety, and *E.* 'Dunkelste Aller' means 'darkest of all', which has deep violet blue flowers. *E.* 'Dominator', a Scottish-bred variety, also has dark flowers that complement the spiky flowers and grey leaves of *Lavandula* beautifully. So too does *E. glaucus* 'Sea Breeze', which I think is my favourite of all.

Eryngium bourgatii 'Picos Amethyst'

Eryngium

(er-*in*-jee-um) (Common name – Sea holly) (Family – Apiaceae)

Type of plant	Hardy, deciduous or evergreen, depending on species
Height/Spread	Up to 90cm/60cm
Flowers/Foliage	'Squashed' globes of tiny blue, metallic flowers surrounded by a ruff of spiky bracts in summer and early autumn/Often spiny or thistle-like, basal, divided grey-green leaves
Best growing conditions	Sun; free-draining, verging on poor, soil
Longevity	Approximately 4 years
Propagation	Seed, as soon as it is ripe; root cuttings, dormant season
Maintenance/Problems	Cut down when flowers and foliage lose their colour/Powdery mildew; blackfly
Good for	Coastal conditions, bees, cutting (be careful of the spines)
Looks good with	*Geranium*, *Verbascum*, *Rudbeckia*, *Verbena*
Selected varieties/cvs	*Eryngium* x *tripartitum* 'Jade Frost' – pale amethyst; *E. bourgatii* 'Oxford Blue'* – blue; *E.* x *zabelii* 'Jos Eijking' – blue; *E. bourgatii* 'Picos Amethyst' – amethyst

I think if you were to try and describe an *Eryngium* to someone who had not seen one, and then went on to say that it is a popular garden plant, you would be looked at in amazement, nay, incredulity! Its thistle-y form and the almost surreal, electric-blue colour of the stems and flowers of some varieties almost defy description, and yet it has established itself as one of the stalwarts of the perennial border. This is perhaps partly due to the fact that there are a couple of British natives (including *E. maritimum*, from which we get the common name of sea holly), which have been cultivated over the years.

Indeed, the long taproot of *E. maritimum* was once candied and sold as sweets (eryngoes), particularly in the Colchester area of Essex – they even get a mention in Shakespeare's *Merry Wives of Windsor* of 1598.

There are dozens of different species of *Eryngium* – all are spectacular in their own way, but I particularly like *E.* x *tripartitum* 'Jade Frost', which has ever-grey, pink-flushed leaves with cream edges and amethyst-coloured flowers. It's a very special variety, which is well worth growing but may be difficult to get hold of unless you go to a specialist nursery.

Eupatorium maculatum Atropurpureum Group

Eupatorium

(yew-pat-*or*-ee-um) (Common name – Joe Pye weed) (Family – Asteraceae)

Type of plant	Hardy, deciduous
Height/Spread	Up to 3m/2m
Flowers/Foliage	Large, domed cluster of small purple-pink flowers in late summer to autumn/Lance-shaped bright green leaves
Best growing conditions	Sun or partial shade; moist soil
Longevity	Approximately 4 years
Propagation	Division, spring or autumn
Maintenance/Problems	Cut back after flowering/Usually trouble-free but can be invasive
Good for	Bees, butterflies, back of border
Looks good with	*Veronicastrum*, *Salvia*, *Campanula*
Selected varieties/cvs	*Eupatorium maculatum* Atropurpureum Group* – purple; *E. maculatum* 'Album' – white; *E. maculatum* Atropurpureum Group 'Purple Bush'* – shorter form (1.5m), light purple

When I lectured at university I heard one of my English literature students describe *Middlemarch* by George Eliot as a 'big book'. This is undoubtedly true, but this description lacked some of the more critical exploration that I was looking for! In a similar vein, I have heard *Eupatorium* described as a big plant. Again, this is correct but it doesn't do it justice. True, it would look a little out of place in a highly manicured, formal setting (a bit like turning up in jeans and T-shirt at a 'posh frock' do) but it is an outstanding plant for the back of a more naturalistic border, flowering in late summer and early autumn when many perennials are past their best. Add to this that it is excellent for pollinating insects, especially bees, and you have a plant that is well worth growing, despite its size.

If you want a shorter plant, try *E. purpureum* subsp. *maculatum* 'Purple Bush', a lovely form raised by Piet Oudolf in Holland. It grows to about 1.5m which is a bit more manageable in the average garden.

As to its common name, Joe Pye weed, I have been unable to discover precisely why it is called this – legend has it that it is named after a Native American who used it to treat typhus.

Euphorbia characias 'Humpty Dumpty'

Euphorbia griffithii 'Dixter'

Euphorbia

(u-*for*-bee-a) (Common name – Spurge) (Family – Euphorbiaceae)

Type of plant	Hardy, deciduous or evergreen, depending on species
Height/Spread	Up to 1.2m/1.2m
Flowers/Foliage	'Inflorescences' rather than flowers, chartreuse with yellow, red or orange tones in late spring and early summer/Lance-shaped bright green, sometimes striped, leaves
Best growing conditions	Various aspects and soil, depending on species
Longevity	Approximately 3 years
Propagation	Seed, as soon as it is ripe; softwood cuttings, spring
Maintenance/Problems	Cut back after flowering/Powdery mildew; aphids; rust
Good for	There is a Euphorbia for every situation! Cut flowers
Looks good with	*Geranium*, *Eremurus*, *Polygonatum*
Selected varieties/cvs	*Euphorbia polychroma** – lime green; *E. griffithii* 'Dixter'* – scarlet; *E. schillingii** – yellow; *E. characias* 'Humpty Dumpty' – lime green
☠ BEWARE ☠	All parts are toxic by ingestion; the white sap from cut stems can cause severe irritation – wash off immediately and keep away from eyes

An episode of the television programme *Gardeners' World* recently featured a chap who was, in his own words, 'euphoric about Euphorbias'. Now I can understand people having passions for things (bees and herbs – oh, and chocolate – do it for me) but – Euphorbias? Try as I might, I can't get very worked up about them, although I can appreciate their merits – very few other plants have varieties that can deal with dry shade at one end of the scale and moist soil in a sunny spot at the other, or have such astonishing chartreuse-coloured 'flowers'. I personally struggle to find room for them in my garden, but that just goes to show how subjective gardening can be.

Were I ever to learn to love them, I think I would go for *E. schillingii*, which is tidier than some and will grow in full sun, or *E.* x *martinii*, which can cope with shady conditions. They are good as cut flowers, so perhaps if I took up flower arranging . . .?

Filipendula palmata

Filipendula rubra 'Venusta'

Filipendula

(fill-ip-*end*-u-la) (Common name – Meadowsweet, Queen of the prairies) (Family – Rosaceae)

Type of plant	Hardy, deciduous
Height/Spread	Up to 1.2m/1m
Flowers/Foliage	Clusters of tiny white or pink flowers in fluffy plumes in summer/Lobed, maple-like green leaves
Best growing conditions	Sun, or can cope with part shade; moist soil
Longevity	Approximately 4 years
Propagation	Division, autumn or spring
Maintenance/Problems	Deadhead regularly/Mildew if too dry
Good for	Damp conditions
Looks good with	*Hosta*, *Echinacea*, *Iris sibirica*
Selected varieties/cvs	*Filipendula rubra* 'Venusta'* – deep rose pink; *F. ulmaria* 'Flora Pleno' – double, white; *F. palmata* – white; *F. purpurea* 'Elegans' – rose pink

Although generally speaking *Filipendula* thrive in moist conditions, the species *F. rubra* can cope with a drier environment, hence its common name of 'Queen of the prairies'. Grown alongside *Echinacea purpurea*, for example, the daisy-like flowers of the *Echinacea* will contrast magnificently with the fluffy, *Astilbe*-like plumes of *F. rubra* 'Venusta'.

In contrast, the species *F. ulmaria* do need moist conditions. I have seen the double form, *F. ulmaria* 'Flora Pleno' grown with a purple *Iris sibirica* (I think it was 'Shirley Pope', but I can't be sure). The dark purple of the *Iris* looked positively regal against the *Filipendula*, while the white 'zone' on the falls of the *Iris* linked with the double white flowers – lovely.

F. ulmaria is the native meadowsweet or meadwort, referring to its use as a flavouring for mead or beer. My beekeeping friend makes mead but I have yet to persuade him to use some meadowsweet in it – in the past, meadowsweet was used for stomach complaints, so I don't think it would do much harm.

Foeniculum vulgare

Foeniculum

(fur-*nik*-u-lum) (Common name – Fennel) (Family – Apiaceae)

Type of plant	Hardy, deciduous
Height/Spread	1.5m/45cm
Flowers/Foliage	Flat-topped umbels of tiny yellow-green flowers in summer/Feathery green leaves
Best growing conditions	Sun; moist but well-drained soil
Longevity	Approximately 3 years
Propagation	Seed, spring; division, spring
Maintenance/Problems	Deadhead regularly/Prolific self-seeder
Good for	Foliage, insects if allowed to flower, as a herb
Looks good with	Just about everything!
Selected varieties/cvs	*Foeniculum vulgare* 'Purpureum' – bronze foliage; *F. vulgare* – green foliage

Fennel is one of those plants that, having been grown for a particular purpose (in this case as a herb) for many years, has now found its way into the herbaceous border, thanks in no small part to its use by designers in gardens at Chelsea and other shows. Fennel's feathery foliage complements anything that is grown alongside it, from *Achillea* to *Veronicastrum*. This is particularly true of the bronze form, *F. vulgare* 'Purpureum', with its maroon/purple-cum-bronze/green foliage.

Fennel grown for its leaves, either as an ornamental in the border or as a herb, should not be confused with Florence fennel (*Foeniculum vulgare* var. *dulce*), primarily grown for its bulbous root. And if you don't want baby *Foeniculum* sprouting up everywhere, be sure to deadhead before they have the chance to shed seed. Indeed some people don't allow the plants to flower at all because the yellow-green flowers often clash with their neighbours. However, if you can tolerate the flowers, they are a beacon for pollinating insects.

Folklore has it that if you hang a bunch of fennel above your door on Midsummer's Eve, you will be protected from enchantment and witches – handy if you are fed up with 'trick-or-treaters' at Hallowe'en!

Gaillardia x *grandiflora* 'Burgunder'

Gaillardia

(gal-*lar*-dee-a) (Common name – Blanket flower) (Family – Asteraceae)

Type of plant	Hardy, deciduous
Height/Spread	60cm/45cm
Flowers/Foliage	Daisy-like flowers in red, yellow, orange/red or yellow/orange, summer and autumn/Basal rosette of hairy green leaves
Best growing conditions	Sun; moderately fertile, well-drained soil
Longevity	Approximately 3 years
Propagation	Division, spring; root cuttings dormant season
Maintenance/Problems	Deadhead regularly; cut down to 15cm after flowering/Downy mildew; slugs
Good for	Bees, cutting
Looks good with	*Helianthus*, *Aster*, *Aconitum*
Selected varieties/cvs	*Gaillardia* x *grandiflora* 'Dazzler'* – orange-red centre tipped with yellow; G. x *grandiflora* 'Burgunder' – deep wine red; G. x *grandiflora* 'St Clements' – peach-orange tipped with yellow

There is no doubt how *Gaillardia* got its Latin designation: it is named after an 18th-century French magistrate, M. Gaillard de Charentonneau, who was a patron of botany. However, there is some disagreement as to how it came by its common name of blanket flower. Some people say that it comes from its resemblance to the patterned blankets made by Native Americans in the plant's indigenous home of the Prairie Provinces of the North American continent; others say that it is because of the plant's ability to cover, or blanket, the ground with flowers.

Gaillardia is probably one of the best 'daisy' flowers to plant in a 'hot' border – the colours range from yellow through orange to red. My favourite is *G.* x *grandiflora* 'St Clements', raised by Hardy's Cottage Garden Plants – it's a stunning plant with a subtle peachy orange centre radiating out to yellow.

Gaillardia flowers are not only very long-lasting, they also make ideal cut flowers; if that wasn't enough, they are excellent plants for pollinating insects too!

Gaura lindheimeri 'Gaudi Red'

Gaura

(*gor*-ra) (Common name – none) (Family – Onagraceae)

Type of plant	Hardy, deciduous
Height/Spread	1.2m/90cm
Flowers/Foliage	Airy spikes of white or pink star-shaped flowers in summer and early autumn/Mats of lance-shaped green, purple-tinged or maroon leaves
Best growing conditions	Sun; moist but well-drained soil
Longevity	Approximately 3 years
Propagation	Division, spring; seed, spring
Maintenance/Problems	Cut back in autumn/Usually trouble-free but occasionally downy mildew
Good for	Cutting
Looks good with	*Sedum, Anemone, Achillea, Salvia*
Selected varieties/cvs	*Gaura lindheimeri* 'Gaudi Red' – pink flowers, red foliage; *G. lindheimeri* 'Siskiyou Pink – deep pink; *G. lindheimeri* 'The Bride' – white

Mention the name *Gaura* to even some experienced gardeners and you are often met with a slightly puzzled, questioning expression, but to my mind it is one of the most useful plants to have in the border. Its airy, almost butterfly-like, flowers dance above the attractive foliage for weeks on end, adding a lightness to the planting without being too 'frothy'. Of course it is not perfect: it can be a little lax in its habit, tapping nearby plants on the shoulder and edging into their space, and given the wrong sort of soil (it has to be really free-draining) it will sulk and soon give up the ghost, but despite these minor undesirable traits it is well worth growing.

I first came across *Gaura* when I was a guest at a wedding, many years ago: both bride and groom were avid gardeners and alongside everyone's place card on the wedding breakfast table was a packet of seeds, each having something to do with weddings – mine was a packet of *G. lindheimeri* 'The Bride'. It was a lovely memento, and I still have the progeny of one of my 'wedding' plants in my garden – a constant reminder of my dear friends.

Geranium sanguineum 'Elke'

Geranium sylvaticum 'Mayflower'

Geranium pratense

Geranium

(jer-*a*-nee-um) (Common name – Cranesbill) (Family – Geraniaceae)

Type of plant	Hardy, deciduous or evergreen, depending on species
Height/Spread	Average 50cm/45cm
Flowers/Foliage	White to purple-red flowers with 5 petals (usually single) in late spring to autumn, depending on species/Divided, mostly green leaves
Best growing conditions	Sun to shade, depending on species; most prefer moist but well-drained soil
Longevity	Approximately 4 years
Propagation	Division, spring or autumn
Maintenance/Problems	Cut back after flowering/Mildew; vine weevil; slugs; snails
Good for	There is a *Geranium* for just about any situation
Looks good with	Almost anything!
Selected varieties/cvs	Too many to mention

I have to apologize for being so vague in the information given above: 'depending on species' crops up more than once, and I concede that 'too many to mention' isn't exactly helpful. *Geranium* is such a diverse group of useful and versatile plants that they warrant a volume of their own to do them justice, so anything I say here will sound trite. The most useful advice I can give is to visit a nursery at the time of year when you want a *Geranium* for your planting space and see what is in flower at that time. Have a good look at the description on the label and take note of the habit and planting requirements; if you are still not sure, ask the nursery owner for advice.

I put my nursery-owning friend on the spot and asked her what *Geranium* she would choose for a sunny spot. Without hesitation she went for *G.* 'Johnson's Blue', a tried and tested *Geranium* with elegant leaves and lavender blue flowers that appear from early summer. And if you cut it back after its first flush of flowers, you will get another display later in the season. It is clump-forming, although it can forget its manners and start sprawling a bit, but don't get cross with it because it is so attractive in other ways.

I shall finish this entry by saying that if you don't know what to put in your garden, plant a *Geranium*!

Geum 'Golden Joy'
Geum 'Lady Stratheden'

Geum

(*je*-um) (Common name – Avens) (Family – Rosaceae)

Type of plant	Hardy, deciduous/semi-evergreen
Height/Spread	Up to 60cm/45cm
Flowers/Foliage	Rose-like yellow, orange or scarlet flowers in late spring and summer/Rosettes of hairy, toothed green leaves
Best growing conditions	Sun; moist but well-drained soil
Longevity	Approximately 4 years
Propagation	Division, spring or autumn
Maintenance/Problems	Cut back after flowering/Sawfly; leaf miner; mildew
Good for	Naturalistic planting, single varieties, bees
Looks good with	*Achillea*, *Euphorbia*, *Aquilegia*
Selected varieties/cvs	*Geum* 'Lady Stratheden'* – semi-double, yellow; *G.* 'Prinses Juliana' – semi-double, orange; *G.* 'Marmalade' – single, orangey yellow; *G.* 'Bell Bank' – double, pink; *G.* 'Totally Tangerine' – single, soft tangerine; *G.* 'Golden Joy' – double, orangey yellow

I don't think *Geum* are as widely grown as they once were, which is a pity because they are 'good do-ers', as the saying goes. They provide splashes of colour when other, more flamboyant, perennials haven't yet got their act together; most are well behaved, forming fairly neat clumps; and the single varieties are good for pollinating insects, especially bees.

Even though the orangey colours of some varieties are a little strident, they contrast well with blues and purples, and put *G.* 'Prinses Juliana' against a lime green *Euphorbia* and you have the 'wow' factor in abundance. If that is a little too much, the sunshine yellow of the doyenne of all *Geum*, 'Lady Stratheden', might be more what you are looking for.

If you veer towards pastels there is even a beautiful pink: *G.* 'Bell Bank', which was thought to be lost to cultivation but was reintroduced by Dove Cottage Nursery in Yorkshire – this one favours slight shade.

Despite my opening sentence above, some new *Geum* are being introduced, and one of the best is *G.* 'Totally Tangerine'. Not only is it a beautiful subtle colour, it flowers its socks off for months on end. It was bred by Tim Crowther of Walberton Nursery, in my home village in West Sussex – so no bias there then!

Helenium 'Moerheim Beauty'

Helenium 'Gartensonne'

Helenium

(hel-*ee*-nee-um) (Common name – Sneezeweed) (Family – Asteraceae)

Type of plant	Hardy, deciduous
Height/Spread	Up to 90cm/50cm
Flowers/Foliage	Daisy-like flowers with prominent centre, in yellow, through orange to red, in summer and autumn/Lance-shaped green leaves
Best growing conditions	Sun; moist but well-drained soil
Longevity	Approximately 3 years
Propagation	Division, spring; softwood cuttings, spring
Maintenance/Problems	Benefits from the 'Chelsea chop' (see Glossary, page 228); cut back after flowering; taller varieties may need staking/Slugs; snails; mildew
Good for	Cutting, bees
Looks good with	*Crocosmia*, *Aconitum*, *Dahlia*
Selected varieties/cvs	*Helenium* 'Moerheim Beauty'* – rich orange-red; *H.* 'Gartensonne' – yellow'; *H.* 'Red Jewel' – dusky red; *H.* 'Beatrice' – tawny yellow; *H.* 'Waltraut' – copper orange
☠ BEWARE ☠	All parts are toxic by ingestion; contact with leaves or sap may cause irritation

Helenium comes from North America. There is some discrepancy over the reasons why it acquired its common name of sneezeweed: some people say that the Native Americans dried the leaves to make a snuff which promoted sneezing to get rid of evil spirits inhabiting the body; others say that it is because *Helenium* causes hayfever and sneezing; while others believe it is because it *prevents* hayfever! Take your pick!

Helenium is one of the best plants for a late border: its daisy flowers catch the fading sunlight and make you smile even on the dullest of autumn days. *H.* 'Moerheim Beauty' is perhaps the best known and most widely grown, but there are many other beautiful varieties: I especially like the very early flowering yellow *H.* 'Wyndley'. The vast majority of non-yellow varieties have orange or orangey red tones, but if you are looking for a variety at the bluer end of the red spectrum (rather than the yellow), look no further than *H.* 'Red Jewel': it's a bit less garish and softer on the eye than some.

Helleborus 'Anemone Centre Pink Spotted'

Helleborus

(hel-ee-*bor*-us) (Common name – Hellebore) (Family – Ranunculaceae)

Type of plant	Hardy, deciduous or evergreen, depending on species
Height/Spread	45cm/45cm
Flowers/Foliage	Mainly large, buttercup-like white, pink or purple flowers in late winter and spring/Lobed and toothed, leathery when mature, green leaves
Best growing conditions	Part shade; moist, fertile soil
Longevity	Approximately 4 years
Propagation	Division, late summer; fresh seed, summer
Maintenance/Problems	Clear away dead flowers and foliage after flowering/Slugs; snails; vine weevil; virus
Good for	Woodland edge
Looks good with	*Galanthus*, *Pulmonaria*, *Brunnera*
Selected varieties/cvs	*Helleborus niger** – white; *H.* 'Hillier Hybrids' – various ranging from white to purple; *H.* x *hybridus* Queen Series – various ranging from white to slatey purple; *H. foetidus** – green
☠ **BEWARE** ☠	All parts are toxic by ingestion; contact with leaves may cause irritation

Helleborus are some of the flowers I look forward to seeing each spring: they unfurl their petals in the most inclement of weather, adding a touch of promise of better things to come. The first to appear in my garden are the straightforward *H. niger*: the flowers are sometimes a little shy and reluctant to push their way through the evergreen leaves but are welcome, nonetheless. Later come the *H.* x *hybridus*: these are a bit more assertive and showy with flowers ranging from white through pink to almost purple. Other species that I don't have in my garden include *H. foetidus*, much taller growing plants which, as their name implies, have an unpleasant smell if you bruise the leaves.

The main problem with *Hellebous* is that they are very promiscuous and will cross-breed readily, producing prolific offspring that often bear no resemblance to either of their parents, the origin of their characteristics being lost in their ancestry. If you don't want lots of spurious seedlings popping up, be sure to deadhead.

Hemerocallis 'Stafford'

Hemerocallis 'Golden Chimes'

Hemerocallis

(hem-er-o-*kal*-is) (Common name – Day lily) (Family – Hemerocallidaceae)

Type of plant	Hardy, deciduous or evergreen, depending on species
Height/Spread	Up to 1.2m/60cm
Flowers/Foliage	White, pink, orange, red or purple lily flowers in summer/Long, narrow, green leaves
Best growing conditions	Sun; moist, well-drained soil
Longevity	Approximately 4 years
Propagation	Division, late summer or early autumn
Maintenance/Problems	Clear away dead flowers and foliage after flowering/Slugs; snails; aphids; spider mites; gall midge
Good for	Sunny spots
Looks good with	Almost anything!
Selected varieties/cvs	There are hundreds to choose from; be guided by the RHS and pick one from the list of those that have been given the Award of Garden Merit

The flowers of *Hemerocallis* open for just one day – hence their common name. Many years ago, before I became really interested in gardening, and in perennials in particular, I remember browsing through a plant catalogue (it was back in the days when catalogues were description only, with no colour pictures!) and wondering, why on earth would anyone want to grow a plant whose flowers lasted for only one day? Then I saw a swathe of *Hemerocallis* in the garden of a stately home and my doubt disappeared – what a sight! What is lacking in individual longevity is more than made up for in the sheer number of blooms that each stem produces.

There are, funnily enough, varieties that open just at night – perhaps they should be called night lilies! Again, each flower appears for one night only (sounds like an entertainment celebrity) and exudes the most beautiful honeysuckle-like fragrance, no doubt to attract nocturnal pollinating insects like moths.

There are so many different varieties of *Hemerocallis* to choose from. Unless you have a particular specimen in mind, look for one which has been given the RHS Award of Garden Merit: this way you know you are buying a garden-worthy plant.

Heuchera 'Obsidian'

Heuchera 'Beaujolais'

Heuchera

(*hew*-ker-a) (Common name – none) (Family – Saxifragaceae)

Type of plant	Hardy, evergreen
Height/Spread	Up to 60cm/40cm
Flowers/Foliage	Feathery sprays of tiny white or pink flowers in spring and summer/Mounds of rounded, heart-shaped or lobed foliage in varying colours
Best growing conditions	Sun to light shade; moist, well-drained soil
Longevity	Approximately 3 years
Propagation	Division, late summer
Maintenance/Problems	Clear away dead flowers and foliage in autumn/Vine weevil
Good for	Interesting foliage, flowers, bees, cutting
Looks good with	Almost anything!
Selected varieties/cvs	*Heuchera* 'Magic Wand'* – green leaves with pink flowers; *H.* 'Obsidian' – almost black leaves; *H.* 'Beaujolais' – burgundy with a touch of silver leaves; *H.* 'Marmalade' – yellow/bronze leaves

Up until the 1980s *Heuchera* were grown mainly for their stems of dainty flowers which are excellent for cutting (and bees love them too). Since then, and with the advent of two quite distinct plants – one from America named *H. sanguinea* 'Snow Storm', with variegated green and cream leaves, and one from Kew gardens in England named *H. diversifolia* 'Palace Purple' (now named *H. villosa* 'Palace Purple') – there has been a deluge of new cultivars with leaf colour ranging from the deepest purple to the most acid lime green that you can imagine. If you are not sure which to go for, pop along to your local nursery and just pick out any that you like.

The biggest problem with any *Heuchera* is the vine weevil. The little blighters can sniff out a *Heuchera* as effectively as my daughter's terrier can sniff out one of her doggy treats. When you buy any *Heuchera* from a garden centre or nursery, gently (and I mean gently!) pull on the crown of the plant – it should hold firm. If there is any 'give' – or worse still, it comes away in your hand – leave it where it is and advise the nursery owner. Nowadays there are biological controls to deal with this bothersome bug so it is worth treating your plants with one of these.

Hosta 'Blue Cadet'

Hosta sp.

Hosta

(*hos*-ta) (Common name – Plantain lily) (Family – Hostaceae)

Type of plant	Hardy, deciduous
Height/Spread	Up to 1m/75cm, depending on species
Flowers/Foliage	Lily-shaped, white or shades of violet in summer/Mounds of elongated heart-shaped green or variegated leaves
Best growing conditions	Part or dappled shade; moist, humus rich soil
Longevity	Approximately 3 years
Propagation	Division, early spring
Maintenance/Problems	Clear away dead flowers and foliage in autumn/Mainly slugs and snails
Good for	Shade, flower arranging
Looks good with	Any other shade-loving plant
Selected varieties/cvs	Impossible to choose!

There is an amazing range of *Hosta*: from those with leaves no more than 6cm long to those with leaves a whopping 50cm long; some have plain green leaves while others have intricate variegation; some have almost nondescript flowers whereas others have remarkable, very fragrant flowers. Despite the latter, *Hosta* are primarily grown for their foliage. New varieties are being introduced annually, and I have to admit that sometimes I find it difficult to tell my 'Minuteman' from my 'Patriot' – but I am not a *Hosta* aficionado!

The one thing that nearly all of them have in common, though, is their attractiveness to slugs and snails; so much so that a friend of mine plants the perimeter of her vegetable patch with *Hosta* to lure the munching molluscs away from her beloved veg. However, some varieties of *Hosta* with tougher leaves, like *H*. 'Blue Angel' and *H*. 'Sugar and Cream', are fairly slug-resistant, so all is not lost.

I have chickened out when it comes to suggesting which varieties to grow – there are simply too many good specimens. Have a look at your local nursery, or at the website of a specialist *Hosta* grower, and, unless you get hooked on *Hosta*, simply choose the ones you like best.

Iris 'Jane Phillips' (blue) and *Iris* 'Sable' (deep purple)

Iris – bearded

(*i*-ris) (Common name – Iris) (Family – Iridaceae)

Type of plant	Hardy, deciduous
Height/Spread	Up to 1m/75cm, depending on species
Flowers/Foliage	Unmistakable flowers with 3 upright 'standards' and 3 'falls', with tufts of hairs on the 'standards', in a range of colours in late spring and summer/Sword-shaped, green leaves
Best growing conditions	Sun; free-draining soil
Longevity	Approximately 3 years
Propagation	Division, late summer
Maintenance/Problems	Lift and divide rhizomes every 3 years or so/Aphids; slugs; snails
Good for	Sun
Looks good with	Other *Iris*, *Lavandula*
Selected varieties/cvs	*Iris* 'Jeanne Price' – yellow; *I.* 'Sable' – dark purple; *I.* 'Jane Phillips'* – blue; *I.* 'Autumn Riesling' – soft orange; *I.* 'Social Graces' – rosy lilac; *I.* 'Just Jennifer' – white
☠ BEWARE ☠	All parts of the plant are toxic; can cause skin irritation

I have deliberately included two entries for *Iris*: one for bearded and one for beardless. This is because they require quite different growing conditions.

Bearded *Iris* require well-drained ground in a sunny spot – in fact the sunnier the better, because the rhizome delights in a good baking and must never be allowed to be swamped by soil or debris. Bearded *Iris* also like a slightly alkaline soil but this is not essential.

Bearded *Iris* are generally categorized according to their size: they can be as short as 20cm or as tall as a metre, so bear in mind where you want to grow them before you choose which ones to buy.

Iris have flowers like no other plant. I think they look unsurpassed if they are grown in their own bed, their remarkable colours vying to catch your eye. The most spectacular display I have ever seen was at Abbey House Gardens in Malmesbury, home of Ian and Barbara Pollard, where they are grown within box hedging. The pristine geometric edges seemed to suit the upright, almost severe, stance of the *Iris* leaves, and then came the anarchic riot of colour: gold, ruby, sapphire, amethyst, opal – precious jewel colours beyond compare; absolutely stunning.

Iris siberica 'Percheron'

Iris – beardless

(*i*-ris) (Common name – Iris) (Family – Iridaceae)

Type of plant	Hardy, deciduous
Height/Spread	Up to 1m/75cm, depending on species
Flowers/Foliage	Unmistakable flowers with 3 upright 'standards' and 3 'falls', in a range of colours in late spring and summer/Grassy, grey-green leaves
Best growing conditions	Sun, part shade; moisture retentive soil
Longevity	Approximately 3 years
Propagation	Division, autumn or spring
Maintenance/Problems	Clear away spent flowers and foliage in autumn/Slugs; snails
Good for	Damp conditions
Looks good with	*Dicentra*, *Zantadeschia*, *Hosta*
Selected varieties/cvs	*Iris sibirica* 'Pleasures of May' – pale lavender/violet; *I. sibirica* 'Butter and Sugar'* – pale yellow/cream; *I. sibirica* 'Rose Quest' – light magenta; *I. sibirica* 'Perry's Blue' – pale blue; *I. siberica* 'Percheron' – blue-violet
☠ **BEWARE** ☠	All parts of the plant are toxic; can cause skin irritation

Iris sibirica is a less showy species than its bearded cousins, but extremely useful, nonetheless. This *Iris* prefers moist, verging on acid soil and it can cope with part shade – conditions that are the extreme opposite of those favoured by bearded *Iris*.

Although *I. sibirica* are clump-forming, they can multiply at a sometimes alarming rate if they feel at home: they will settle down and stretch out and before you know it they have occupied the space next to theirs that you had allocated for something else – in much the same way as our cat, Mocha, takes up residence on the whole of the settee.

On *I. sibirica* flowers the falls and standards tend to be of the same colour, and the majority are blue, purple, yellow, white and occasionally pink. There are some varieties, however, such as *I. sibirica* 'Salamander Crossing', where the falls and standards are of different colours. Breeders are also creating new varieties with bigger flowers – I haven't quite decided whether I like this trend or not: there is something charming about the smaller flowers hovering like butterflies above the strappy foliage. Maybe we should leave the flowery flamboyance to their cousins, the bearded iris.

Knautia macedonica

Knautia

(*nor*-tee-a) (Common name – none) (Family – Dipsacaceae)

Type of plant	Hardy, deciduous
Height/Spread	Up to 1m/50cm
Flowers/Foliage	Pincushion-like flowers in shades of pink and crimson in early summer to autumn/Jagged, basal, green/grey leaves
Best growing conditions	Sun; light, slightly alkaline soil
Longevity	Approximately 3 years
Propagation	Seed, spring; basal cuttings, spring
Maintenance/Problems	Cut out old stems after flowering/Occasionally aphids
Good for	Cutting, bees, naturalistic planting
Looks good with	Almost anything
Selected varieties/cvs	*Knautia macedonica* – maroon; *K. macedonica* Melton pastels – shades of pink and lavender

Unlike many other perennials, where you can spend hours deliberating over which plant to choose from hundreds of different species and varieties on offer, *Knautia* is a breeze – you can have any species, as long as it's *K. macedonica*, and you can have any colour as long as it's red, pink, lavender, or somewhere in between! (Strictly speaking *K. macedonica* isn't the only species available; there is *K. arvensis*, the native field scabious, but this doesn't often find its way into the perennial border.)

Despite its lack of diversity and natural simplicity, it is a lovely plant to have in the garden: *K. macedonica* is extremely prolific and long-flowering, each plant producing hundreds of little pincushion flowers, each of these lasting up to a fortnight; it is a beacon for nectar-loving insects; it makes a lovely addition to a vase of cut flowers; and, if you leave some seed heads on over the winter, provides welcome food for birds.

I particularly like the straightforward *K. macedonica*, which has rich maroon flowers. The Melton pastels strain has a pleasing mixture of softer, paler colours, but you have to wait until they flower before you know exactly what colour you are getting.

Kniphofia caulescens

Kniphofia 'Bees' Lemon'

Kniphofia 'Toffee Nosed'

Kniphofia

(ni-*fo*-fee-a) (Common name – Red hot poker) (Family – Asphodelaceae)

Type of plant	Hardy, deciduous (occasionally evergreen)
Height/Spread	Up to 1.5m/75cm
Flowers/Foliage	Spikes of long, tubular, orange, yellow or cream flowers in summer and autumn/Rosettes of thin, spiky green leaves
Best growing conditions	Sun; fertile, well-drained soil
Longevity	Approximately 4 years
Propagation	Division, spring or autumn
Maintenance/Problems	Cut back flowering stem after flowering/Usually trouble-free but detests wet soil in winter
Good for	Nectar-loving insects
Looks good with	*Aconitum*, *Echinacea*, *Rudbeckia*
Selected varieties/cvs	*Kniphofia* 'Little Maid' – green/cream; *K.* 'Toffee Nosed'* – orange/cream; *K.* 'Brimstone'* – yellow; *K.* 'Bees' Lemon' – yellow

Neither the common name nor the botanical name has endeared *Kniphofia* to the average gardener: indeed it was, and still is on occasions, deemed to be vulgar, indicating a lack of good taste. Well, call me tasteless, but I rather like *Kniphofia* – it provides a really useful 'punctuation mark' in the herbaceous border, every bit as good as *Verbascum* or *Delphinium*.

At one time the only *Kniphofia* that seemed to be available had rather garish orange/red flowers, resembling – yes, you've guessed – a red hot poker! Nowadays, however, there are lots of new varieties which are more subtle and less brash than the old-fashioned one. *K.* 'Little Maid', for example, introduced by Beth Chatto, has flowers that start pale green, then fade to cream. The leaves are narrow and neat, and it's a short variety, rarely growing more than 60cm tall. Two other favourites are *K.* 'Toffee Nosed', which has tawny orange flowers fading to cream, and the aptly named *K.* 'Brimstone', which has green buds opening to sulphur yellow flowers.

As well as providing statuesque vertical interest in the border, *Kniphofia* also produce so much nectar that you can actually see it seeping out of the tubular flowers, especially *K. caulescens* – a real feast for insects, and especially wasps, so take care.

Lamium – various species

Lamium 'Lami Pink'

Lamium

(*lam*-ee-um) (Common name – Dead nettle) (Family – Lamiaceae)

Type of plant	Hardy, evergreen
Height/Spread	25cm/60cm
Flowers/Foliage	Spikes of purplish pink, pink or white 2-lipped flowers in summer and autumn/Pairs of heart-shaped or oval, toothed, green or variegated leaves
Best growing conditions	Shade or part shade, will tolerate some sun; moist soil
Longevity	Approximately 4 years
Propagation	Division, spring or autumn; rooted stems, any time during growing season
Maintenance/Problems	Clear away dead leaves and flowers in autumn/Usually trouble-free
Good for	Nectar-loving insects, ground cover, shady spots
Looks good with	*Aquilegia*, *Helleborus*, spring flowering bulbs
Selected varieties/cvs	*Lamium maculatum* 'White Nancy'* – white; *L. maculatum* 'Pink Nancy' – pink; *L. maculatum* 'Pink Pewter' – salmon pink; *L. maculatum* 'Beacon Silver' – pink/purple; *L.* 'Lami Pink' – pink-purple

It's a shame that this lovely little plant's common name is dead nettle. It's so uninspiring and, frankly, dull. Why couldn't it be called 'bee sup' (bees love it) or 'kiss-me-quick' (the flowers have two lips) – I feel certain it would increase its popularity! But it's stuck with dead nettle and has to make the best of it.

Plant breeders seem to be making the best of it, though, with lots of variegated forms finding their way into nurseries and garden centres. Among the prettiest is *Lamium maculatum* 'Pink Nancy', which has leaves that aren't too stridently variegated, and flowers the most beautiful shade of salmon pink perched above the foliage.

I find the variegation of some a little too uneasy on the eye but they will certainly brighten up a shady corner of the garden, forming a mat of green and cream or gold where other plants would struggle to cope.

Lathyrus grandiflorus

Lathyrus

(*lath*-ee-rus) (Common name – Sweet pea) (Family – Papilionaceae)

Type of plant	Hardy, deciduous
Height/Spread	Up to 2m/45cm
Flowers/Foliage	Familiar, winged flowers, white or shades of pink and magenta in summer and autumn/Oval green leaflets with (usually) tendrils
Best growing conditions	Sun; rich, well-drained soil
Longevity	Approximately 3 years
Propagation	Division, spring
Maintenance/Problems	Deadhead frequently; needs support/Aphids; mildew
Good for	Climbing
Looks good with	*Delphinium, Helianthus, Anemone*
Selected varieties/cvs	*Lathyrus latifolius** – purplish pink; *L. latifolius* 'Albus'* – white; *L. latifolius* 'White Pearl'* – white; *L. grandiflorus* – violet/pink

The perennial sweet peas *Lathyrus latifolius* and *L. grandiflorus* are very similar to the well-known annual *L. odoratus*, but there are some notable differences. The obvious one is that the perennial sweet peas will last more than a year; another is that the flowers of the perennial species are not as varied in colour, or as large, as the annual ones; and, disappointingly, the perennial flowers have no fragrance. Given the right conditions, they can be a little invasive, too. In many areas they have escaped from the garden and established themselves in hedgerows and on fertile waste ground. They haven't got to the stage of making a nuisance of themselves, however, so don't be dissuaded from growing them in your own garden.

Of the few cultivars that are available, I particularly like *L. latifolius* 'White Pearl' with its pure white, slightly larger, flowers. It doesn't have the same desire to muscle in on its neighbours as some of the others, and it Looks good with whatever you put it with – it's especially useful for scrambling through shrubs or as a backdrop to a border.

Lavandula angustifolia

Lavandula sp.

Lavandula

(lav-*an*-dew-la) (Common name – Lavender) (Family – Lamiaceae)

Type of plant	Hardy, evergreen shrub
Height/Spread	Up to 1m/45cm
Flowers/Foliage	Spikes of lipped, purple, lavender, pink or white fragrant flowers in summer/Aromatic, lance-shaped, narrow grey-green leaves
Best growing conditions	Sun; well-drained soil
Longevity	Approximately 4 years
Propagation	Semi-ripe cuttings, summer
Maintenance/Problems	Cut back after flowering/Usually trouble-free
Good for	Bees, cutting, drying
Looks good with	Almost anything!
Selected varieties/cvs	*Lavandula angustifolia* 'Hidcote* – deep purple; *L. angustifolia* 'Blue Mountain White' – pure white; *L. angustifolia* 'Rosea' – pale pink; *L. angustifolia* 'Betty's Blue' – purple

Strictly speaking, *Lavandula* should not be included in this book. It is a shrub, not a herbaceous perennial. It is so often used as a perennial, however, that I feel justified in stretching the rules a little and letting it join the club as an honorary member.

There are many kinds of *Lavandula* but if you want them to act as a perennial you must grow the hardy kind. The hardiest are undoubtedly *L. angustifolia* and *L.* x *intermedia* (*L. stoechas* – the one with 'bunny ears' – is borderline hardy). Even within these two groups there are dozens of varieties, but you would be hard pressed to do better than *L. angustifolia* 'Hidcote' – a rich, dark purple lavender that grows to about 50cm. The main problem with 'Hidcote' is that there are so many imposters: if you want the genuine article, be sure to buy from a specialist lavender nursery.

There is so much to like about lavender: it's relatively easy to grow; it is a superb bee plant; lavender flowers can be used in cooking, in both savoury and sweet dishes; the dried flowers can be put in lavender bags to fragrance linen and to deter moths; it has medicinal uses; and, finally, its oil is essential in many perfumes. There are very few plants that can claim to do all those things and still look beautiful!

There are, however, a couple of things to remember when growing lavender. First, it needs really good drainage and a sheltered spot; and second, when you cut it back, be sure not to go too far into the old wood, otherwise it will not regenerate.

Leucanthemum x superbum 'T E Killin'

Leucanthemum x superbum

Leucanthemum

(lew-*kan*-the-mum) (Common name – Shasta daisy) (Family – Asteraceae)

Type of plant	Hardy, deciduous
Height/Spread	Up to 1m/60cm
Flowers/Foliage	Daisy flowers in white, cream or yellow with yellow centre, in summer and early autumn/Lobed or divided, dark green leaves
Best growing conditions	Sun; fertile, well-drained soil
Longevity	Approximately 3 years
Propagation	Division, late summer or early spring
Maintenance/Problems	Benefits from the 'Chelsea chop' (see Glossary, page 228); deadhead regularly; taller varieties may need staking/Slugs; snails; aphids
Good for	Cutting
Looks good with	*Achillea, Agastache, Knautia, Echinops, Kniphofia*
Selected varieties/cvs	*Leucanthemum* x *superbum* 'T E Killin'* – white; *L.* x *superbum* 'Sonnenschein' – primrose yellow; *L.* x *superbum* 'Banana Cream' – lemon yellow; *L.* x *superbum* 'Phyllis Smith' – white

The daisy flowers of *Leucanthemum* range from the newly combed, not-a-hair-out-of-place type, to the scruffy, dragged-through-a-hedge-backwards, bad-hair-day type. I rather like both – depending on how compliant or rebellious I feel on the day! Whatever their individual nuances, their fundamental shape complements so many other flower forms, from the flat heads of *Achillea* to the torch-like spikes of *Kniphofia*, that they look good in any border.

The best method of propagation is by division. You can raise new plants from seed, which make lovely dwarf specimens, flowering in the first year: they then grow much bigger in subsequent years, so be careful where you position them to begin with. Plants raised from seed that you have collected yourself are often variable and do not come true.

Liatris spicata

Liatris

(lee-*at*-riss) (Common name – Gay feather) (Family – Asteraceae)

Type of plant	Hardy, deciduous
Height/Spread	Up to 90cm/45cm
Flowers/Foliage	Spikes of pink, purple or white flowers in late summer/Basal tuft of narrow, green leaves which extend up the flower stem
Best growing conditions	Sun; moisture retentive but well-drained soil
Longevity	Approximately 3 years
Propagation	Division, early spring; seed, autumn
Maintenance/Problems	Deadhead regularly; taller varieties may need staking/Rust
Good for	Cutting, bees, drying, 'meadow' planting
Looks good with	*Achillea, Agastache, Echinops, Leucanthemum*
Selected varieties/cvs	*Liatris spicata* – pinkish purple; *L. spicata* 'Kobold' – rose pink; *L. spicata* 'Floristan Weiss' – white; *L. spicata* 'Floristan Violett' – violet

The most noticeable thing about *Liatris* is that the flowers, arranged around the poker-like stem, open from the top down. This is quite a novelty in the horticultural world, which is why, I suspect, some varieties have been developed specifically to use as cut flowers: it's much nicer to see open flowers protruding from a bunch than tight, colourless buds. The Floristan Series have a shorter stem, but with more flowers, so if you want to grow your flowers for cutting, these are the ones to choose. You can grow them from seed, and when the time comes to cut them, wait until about half the flowers are open.

They look equally good in the garden, however, providing a useful vertical element in the border. I like to plant them alongside *Allium* to give a continuity of 'punctuation marks', leading the eye through the planting: when the *Allium* are going over, the *Liatris* are just starting to come into their own.

Ligularia 'The Rocket'

Ligularia

(lig-yew-*lair*-ee-a) (Common name – Leopard plant) (Family – Asteraceae)

Type of plant	Hardy, deciduous
Height/Spread	Up to 2m/1m
Flowers/Foliage	Spikes of yellow or orange daisy-like flowers in summer/Kidney -shaped or elliptical green leaves, often divided or toothed
Best growing conditions	Part shade; rich, moist soil
Longevity	Approximately 3 years
Propagation	Division, spring or autumn
Maintenance/Problems	Clear away spent flowers and leaves/Slugs; snails
Good for	Damp situations
Looks good with	*Persicaria*, *Zantedeschia*, *Astilbe*
Selected varieties/cvs	*Ligularia* 'Gregynog Gold'* – orange-yellow; *L. przewalskii** – yellow; *L.* 'The Rocket' – yellow; *L. dentata* 'Desdemona'* – orange; *L. hodgsonii* – yellow

If you have a damp spot in part shade in your garden and are fed up with ferns, don't despair! *Ligularia* could be the answer: they revel in moist soil, really don't like the sun, and have bright, cheery flowers to perk up a dull spot. The major drawback is that most reach statuesque dimensions, filling their allocated space and dominating their neighbours, so you need to give them room to reach their potential. You can keep them within bounds, however, by digging them up and dividing them periodically.

If your garden would struggle to accommodate any of the more well-known species, it is worth searching for *Ligularia hodgsonii*, which is a more compact species from Japan, reaching a modest 90cm. It is not as readily available as some but a specialist perennial nursery would do their best to source it for you.

Lobelia x *speciosa* 'Fan Scharlach'

Lobelia x *speciosa* 'Fan Burgundy'

Lobelia x *speciosa* 'Fan Blau'

Lobelia

(lo-*bee*-lee-a) (Common name – none) (Family – Campanulaceae)

Type of plant	Hardy, deciduous
Height/Spread	Up to 90cm/45cm
Flowers/Foliage	Spikes of tubular and lobed flowers in various colours ranging from red to purple in summer and early autumn/Narrow green or purple leaves
Best growing conditions	Sun; rich, moist soil
Longevity	Approximately 3 years
Propagation	Division, spring
Maintenance/Problems	Clear away spent flowers and leaves/Slugs; virus
Good for	Pollinating insects, cottage garden
Looks good with	*Kniphofia*, *Helenium*, *Achillea*
Selected varieties/cvs	*Lobelia* x *speciosa* 'Hadspen Purple' – purple; *L.* x *speciosa* 'Pink Flamingo' – pink; *L.* x *speciosa* Fan Series – various; *L. cardinalis** – scarlet
☠ BEWARE ☠	With the exception of annual bedding Lobelia, all species are poisonous; sap will cause irritation to the skin and eyes

If you mention *Lobelia*, most people will immediately think of the blue annual bedding plants that often edge summer borders of *Pelargonium* and *Antirrhinum*, or the trailing variety that adorn many a hanging basket, flowering their little socks off all summer long.

There are, however, perennial species that are quite different in stature from their annual cousins and are, arguably, even more valuable in the garden, especially if you have rich, deep soil that holds the moisture without being sodden. One of the most arresting species is *L. cardinalis* with, not surprisingly, scarlet flowers: it also has reddish purple stems and bronze-tinted leaves – a combination that is striking without being sombre.

Lobelia are named after Matthias de l'Obel, a plant collector who also served as physician to King James I. L'Obel is credited with being the first botanist to try to classify plants according to their natural propensities, rather than their medicinal uses: this was a century before Karl Linnaeus worked on the same problem and who devised the system for the naming of plants that we still use today.

Lupinus nootkatensis

Lupinus sp.

Lupinus

(lu-*py*-nus) (Common name – Lupin) (Family – Papilionaceae)

Type of plant	Hardy, deciduous
Height/Spread	Up to 1m/50cm
Flowers/Foliage	Dense spikes of pea-like flowers in various colours, often bi-coloured, in summer/Basal mounds of finger-like green leaves
Best growing conditions	Sun; well-drained, slightly acid soil
Longevity	Approximately 4 years
Propagation	Careful division, spring; basal cuttings, late spring; seed, spring or autumn (see below)
Maintenance/Problems	Clear away spent flowers and leaves/Slugs; aphids
Good for	Cottage garden
Looks good with	*Achillea, Aquilegia, Campanula*
Selected varieties/cvs	*Lupinus* Band of Nobles Series*, including 'Chandelier' – yellow, 'The Chatelaine' – pink/white; *L. nootkatensis* – purple/blue; *L.* 'Persian Slipper' – blue/white
☠ BEWARE ☠	Although some species are used as animal fodder, others are toxic, so treat with caution; do not ingest

A friend of mine loves lupins so much that each year, when I ask what he would like for his birthday, his answer is always 'lupins'. One year I grew a tray-full of mixed Band of Nobles Series – 30 in total – from seed sown the previous year, and he was as happy as a bee in a honey pot. If you use seed, the important thing to remember is to soak them for 24 hours before sowing them: this aids germination no end.

I can't say that I am as enthusiastic about *Lupinus* as my friend, but I do like some of the single-coloured varieties, particularly *Lupinus* 'Chandelier' in shades of yellow, and the species *L. nootkatensis*.

Being a member of the legume clan (like peas and beans), *Lupinus* have the ability to fix nitrogen in the soil by means of their root nodules, and are sometimes grown as a green manure. In addition, because (being legumes) the seeds are highly nutritious, some species are once again being grown as animal fodder. Please don't be tempted to try them for yourself – some species are toxic: be content to grow them for the colourful flowers.

Lysimachia punctata

Lysimachia

(lis-em-*ack*-ee-a) (Common name – Loosestrife) (Family – Primulaceae)

Type of plant	Hardy, deciduous
Height/Spread	Up to 1m/50cm
Flowers/Foliage	Spikes of (usually) yellow flowers in summer/Lance-shaped or elliptical pairs or clusters of 3 or 4 green leaves
Best growing conditions	Sun or part shade; moist soil
Longevity	Approximately 4 years
Propagation	Division, spring; seed, spring
Maintenance/Problems	Cut back in autumn/Usually trouble-free; some species can be invasive
Good for	Damp situations
Looks good with	*Astilbe*, *Iris*
Selected varieties/cvs	*Lysimachia punctata* – yellow; *L. punctata* 'Alexander' – yellow flowers, variegated leaves; *L. atropurpurea* 'Beaujolais' – burgundy; *L. ephemerum* – white

In polite society *Lysimachia* is described as robust or uncomfortably vigorous; the not so charitable call it a thug. It is true that some species can get a bit too big for their boots and start throwing their weight around, but they are useful plants for damp situations.

The most common garden species is *L. punctata* with its yellow, cup-shaped flowers; a less energetic choice is the variegated *L. punctata* 'Alexander'. Also worth considering are *L. atropurpurea* 'Beaujolais' and *L. ephemerum*, both of which have smaller and daintier flowers than *L. punctata*. They are also less invasive than *L. punctata*, and this, to my mind, makes them more able to be accommodated into a planting scheme.

Malva sylvestris 'Blue Fountain'

Malva moschata f. *alba*

Malva moschata

Malva

(*mal*-va) (Common name – Mallow) (Family – Malvaceae)

Type of plant	Hardy, deciduous
Height/Spread	Up to 90cm/50cm
Flowers/Foliage	Spikes of five-petalled, open pink, lavender or violet flowers in summer/Alternate round, heart-shaped or lobed green leaves
Best growing conditions	Sun; fairly fertile, well-drained soil
Longevity	Approximately 4 years
Propagation	Basal cuttings, spring; seed, spring
Maintenance/Problems	Cut back main stem after flowering; tidy up in autumn/Aphids; rust
Good for	Insects
Looks good with	*Anemone, Penstemon, Agastache, Knautia*
Selected varieties/cvs	*Malva moschata* f. *alba** – silver pink; *M. moschata* f. *rosea* – deep pink; *M. alcea* var. *fastigiata* – deep pink; *M. sylvestris* 'Blue Fountain' – blue purple

Look at the flowers of *Malva* and it is easy to see how they belong to the same family as *Alcea* (hollyhocks), *Althaea* and *Lavatera* – all of which could be reasonably described, I think, as old-fashioned plants, which tend not to find their way into modern planting schemes. But *Malva* have much to commend them: their simple charm is an asset in many situations, especially if you are looking for a 'cottage' or naturalistic feel to your garden; they attract a wide range of beneficial insects; and the flowers fade gracefully, even the white form, *M. moschata* f. *alba*, which has a tinge of pink to it, making it less hard on the eye than other, more strident whites.

In fact, of all the *Malva* I think the white form is the best, and I wouldn't be without it somewhere in my garden; perhaps this is because it reminds me of an old lady who used to live in our village when I was young. She always had a bag of marshmallows in her pocket and gave us one whenever we saw her. She told us that she made them from her marshmallow bush, pointing towards the white-flowered plant next to her front door. I found out much later that 'her' plant was in fact *M. moschata* f. *alba*, whereas marshmallows are made from the root of *Althaea officinalis* – besides which, her marshmallows looked remarkably similar to the ones Mr Joe sold at the village shop ... But the association lives on in my mind.

Monarda 'Aquarius'

Monarda 'Gardenview Scarlet'

Monarda

(mon-*ar*-da) (Common name – Bergamot, Bee balm) (Family – Lamiaceae)

Type of plant	Hardy, deciduous
Height/Spread	Up to 90cm/50cm
Flowers/Foliage	Tubular 'shaggy' heads of white, through pink to red flowers with coloured bracts in summer/Opposite pairs of toothed, lance-shaped or oval green leaves, often with a purple tinge
Best growing conditions	Sun or part shade; moisture retentive, free-draining soil
Longevity	Approximately 3 years
Propagation	Division, spring; cuttings, spring; species by seed, spring
Maintenance/Problems	Deadhead regularly; cut back in autumn/Powdery mildew
Good for	Bees, butterflies, cutting
Looks good with	*Verbascum*, *Eryngium*, *Echinops*, *Phlox*
Selected varieties/cvs	*Monarda didyma* – red; *M.* 'Gardenview Scarlet'* – red; *M.* 'Schneewittchen' – white; and see below

Many people are put off growing *Monarda* because of their susceptibility to powdery mildew. This is indeed an annoying affliction and although many cultivars are advertised as being 'resistant', it really all depends on a whole raft of factors from weather and density of planting to the particular strain of mildew. Dutch nurseryman Piet Oudolf has come up with a couple of strains that demonstrate more resistance than others: the first is a group with Native American resonances – for example, 'Squaw' and 'Mohawk'; the other group were originally named after zodiac signs but many have since been renamed – for example, 'Scorpion' (formerly 'Scorpio') and 'Fishes' ('Pisces').

Even if your *Monarda* do succumb to mildew they are well worth growing because their 'bad-hair-day' flowers not only add an interesting form to the border, they also provide nectar for bees and butterflies.

The minty, slightly spicy leaves of the species *M. didyma* can be made into a tisane. In fact in North America, where the species originates, the Native Americans have long used it for medicinal purposes. The early settlers learned about this and named the plant 'Oswego Tea' after the Oswego Native Americans who introduced them to it. The first written account of it is by a Spanish physician, Nicholas Monardes (hence the plant's name) in the sixteenth century.

Nepeta racemosa 'Walker's Low'

Nepeta hybrida 'Pink Candy'

Nepeta

(nep-*ee*-ta) (Common name – Catmint) (Family – Lamiaceae)

Type of plant	Hardy, deciduous
Height/Spread	Up to 90cm/45cm
Flowers/Foliage	Spikes or clusters of tubular, 2-lipped, usually blue flowers, in early summer to autumn/Pairs of oval, sometimes toothed, grey-green leaves
Best growing conditions	Sun; free-draining soil
Longevity	Approximately 4 years
Propagation	Division, spring; softwood cuttings, summer
Maintenance/Problems	Cut back in autumn/Powdery mildew; slugs; and cats!
Good for	Bees
Looks good with	*Allium*, *Eryngium*, *Verbascum*, *Rosa*
Selected varieties/cvs	*Nepeta* 'Six Hills Giant' – lavender blue; *N. racemosa* 'Little Titch' – lavender blue; *N. racemosa* 'Snowflake' – white; *N. racemosa* 'Walker's Low' – violet blue; *N. hybrida* 'Pink Candy' – pink

Nepeta isn't called catmint for nothing! I have covered mine with a woven cloche, sprinkled lion poo around it, even encircled it with a line of *Coleus canina* (the 'scaredy cat' plant) to try and deter our cat, Mocha, from pouncing on it, chewing it and generally destroying it. All to no avail. Apparently *Nepeta* contains the chemical nepetalactone, which is irresistible to many cats. Reluctantly, I have conceded defeat.

If you have a cat-less garden, or your cat is one of the few that show no interest in it, *Nepeta* is a lovely plant to have in your garden, especially if you want to attract bees. The most widely available is *N.* 'Six Hills Giant' which, as its name suggests, grows pretty tall – up to 90cm. It can be a little unruly, slouching over its neighbours if not supported. A shorter version is *N. racemosa* 'Walker's Low', a more upright, modest plant reaching about 60cm. If you want something even more compact then go for *N. racemosa* 'Little Titch', a charming, floriferous version that grows to little more than 15cm.

The shorter varieties of *Nepeta* make good edging plants. I have seen it used in place of *Lavandula* to good effect, but the aroma isn't quite as attractive.

Origanum sp.

Origanum

(or-ree-*gar*-num) (Common name – Oregano) (Family – Lamiaceae)

Type of plant	Hardy, deciduous or evergreen, depending on species
Height/Spread	Up to 60cm/30cm
Flowers/Foliage	Clusters of tubular, lipped, pink or white flowers, in summer and autumn/Pairs of oval, green or yellow-green leaves
Best growing conditions	Sun; free-draining soil
Longevity	Approximately 4 years
Propagation	Division, spring; softwood cuttings, summer
Maintenance/Problems	Cut back in spring/Usually trouble-free
Good for	Bees and other pollinating insects
Looks good with	*Anthemis*, *Sedum*, *Lavandula*
Selected varieties/cvs	*Origanum laevigatum* 'Herrenhausen'* – mauve-pink; *O. laevigatum* 'Purple Charm' – purple; *O. vulgare* 'Thumble's Variety' – white flowers, greenish-yellow leaves; *O. vulgare* 'Country Cream' – pink, leaves green edged with cream

There are many species of *Origanum* but the two most widely grown in the herbaceous border are *O. laevigatum* and *O. vulgare.* The latter is the well-known culinary herb, which if allowed to flower has dainty pink blossoms that are very attractive to bees and other pollinating insects: the nectar contains a whopping 76% sugar! There are many cultivars within this group that are garden-worthy, particularly the variegated forms and those with yellow-green leaves.

Unlike *O. vulgare*, *O. laevigatum* is purely decorative: neither the leaves nor the flowers are edible. More positively, it contains varieties with much showier flowers that are, arguably, better suited to a border situation. Among them are *O. laevigatum* 'Herrenhausen', which has purple-flushed leaves and a profusion of mauve-pink flowers – a real show-stopper, especially when it's covered in bees of all descriptions busily collecting nectar.

Paeonia lactiflora 'Shirley Temple'

Paeonia

(pee-*o*-nee-a) (Common name – Peony) (Family – Peoniaceae)

Type of plant	Hardy, deciduous
Height/Spread	Up to 1m/80cm
Flowers/Foliage	Showy, single or double rose-like flowers in white, shades of pink and red in early and mid-summer, depending on variety/Leaves consisting of 9 or more leaflets, often emerging with reddish tones which then turn green
Best growing conditions	Sun; free-draining soil
Longevity	Approximately 5 years
Propagation	Division, autumn
Maintenance/Problems	Cut back in late autumn; tall varieties may need support/Blight; virus diseases
Good for	The 'wow' factor, cutting
Looks good with	*Geranium*, *Campanula*, *Delphinium*
Selected varieties/cvs	Too many to choose! The most popular are *Paeonia lactiflora* 'Duchesse de Nemours'* – double, white; *P. lactiflora* 'Sarah Bernhardt'* – double, apple-blossom pink; *P. lactiflora* 'Bowl of Beauty'* – 'open' double, mid pink; *P.* 'Buckeye Belle' – semi-double, russet red

A garden full of *Paeonia* is a fairly fleeting joy, although you can extend the season and get a succession of flowers from May to July if you plant several varieties. What they lack in flowering longevity, however, they more than make up for in their 'wow' factor. Even the single flowers are unashamedly showy, but for flagrant floral flamboyance, go for the double varieties – spectacular, verging on ostentatious, these beauties steal the show every time.

Like many celebrities, they have a reputation of being 'difficult'. True, they can sulk a little and have exacting requirements, but no more so than some other perennials. There are a few things to bear in mind, however: they do not thrive in pots; they hate wet soil; plant them in a good-sized hole with plenty of organic matter in the bottom, so that the crown is about 5cm below the surface – mulch, but do not cover the crown; move or divide them in autumn. This may sound a lot of bother, but the effort will be repaid many-fold.

Papaver orientale 'Patty's Plum'

Papaver

(*pap*-a-ver) (Common name – Poppy) (Family – Papaveraceae)

Type of plant	Hardy, deciduous
Height/Spread	Up to 90cm/50cm
Flowers/Foliage	Delicate cupped or saucer-shaped single or double flowers in white, shades of pink, purple and red in summer/Basal tufts of bristly lobed or toothed green leaves
Best growing conditions	Sun; moisture retentive but free-draining soil
Longevity	Approximately 4 years
Propagation	Root cuttings, dormant season; seed rarely comes true
Maintenance/Problems	Clear away spent foliage and flowers; tall varieties will need support/Powdery mildew
Good for	The 'wow' factor
Looks good with	*Geranium*, *Allium*, *Delphinium*, *Campanula*; fill the gaps after flowering with *Penstemon*
Selected varieties/cvs	Almost any from the Oriental Poppy Group, including *Papaver* 'Bolero' – dusky pink; *P.* 'Beauty of Livermere' – crimson-scarlet; *P.* 'Royal Wedding' – white; *P.* 'Patty's Plum' – purple

Until fairly recently poppies in the Oriental Poppy Group were listed under *Papaver orientale*. However, the majority appear to be hybrids rather than true offspring of the species, hence the new collective name of Oriental Poppy Group. I wouldn't mind betting that many garden centres and nurseries will continue to list them as *P. orientale*, though.

Either way, the majority of perennial poppies that are grown in the garden belong to this group, and although fleeting, their delicate, silk-like flowers grace the border like no other. I am a sucker for their butterfly-like emergence from cocooned buds, crumpled petals unfurling like wings. I particularly like *P.* 'Bolero', a dusky pink, less sombre than *P.* 'Patty's Plum' but every bit as good.

After flowering, the foliage will die back to nothing, to reappear later in the summer. Although the seed heads look spectacular it is as well to remove them before they have a chance to shed seed: the resulting babies rarely look like their parents and for every one half-decent progeny you will end up with hundreds that aren't worth soil space.

Penstemon 'Blackberry Fancy'

Penstemon 'Blueberry Fudge'

Penstemon hartwegii 'Tubular Bells Pink'

Penstemon 'Bubble Gum'

Penstemon

(pen-*stem*-on) (Common name – none) (Family – Scrophulariaceae)

Type of plant	Hardy (see below), evergreen
Height/Spread	Up to 1m/50cm
Flowers/Foliage	Spikes of tubular or bell-shaped flowers in pink, purple, red and white in summer and into autumn/Narrow, lance-shaped, green leaves
Best growing conditions	Sun; rich but free-draining soil
Longevity	Approximately 4 years
Propagation	Cuttings, spring or autumn
Maintenance/Problems	Deadhead regularly; cut back old growth in spring, not autumn/Powdery mildew; slugs; aphids; eelworm
Good for	Bees, cutting
Looks good with	*Achillea, Phlox, Echinacea, Perovskia*
Selected varieties/cvs	*Penstemon* 'Andenken an Friedrich Hahn'* – crimson; *P.* 'Evelyn'* – mid pink; *P.* 'Stapleford Gem'* – pale lilac blue; *P. hartwegii* Tubular Bells Series; *P.* Ice Cream Series, such as *P.* 'Bubble Gum'

There tends to be some controversy over the hardiness of *Penstemon*. Some plants succumb to winter weather, while others of the same variety may survive – and this can happen when they are all growing in the same garden! Much depends on a raft of different factors – weather, soil, shelter, and so on. But it seems to be winter wetness that is more damaging than plunging temperatures. Insurance is the best policy with *Penstemon* – take cuttings and keep them over winter in a protected, but not necessarily heated, environment, just in case the parent plants don't make it.

Of all *Penstemon*, *P.* 'Andenken an Friedrich Hahn' (syn. *P.* 'Garnet') seems to be the hardiest but there are so many other attractive cultivars that it's worth taking a chance. I particularly like the colours that veer towards purple, like *P.* 'Blackberry Fancy' and *P.* 'Blueberry Fudge'.

You can also get *Penstemon* that flower in their first year even when they have been grown from seed. I tried *P. hartwegii* 'Tubular Bells Rose'. They took longer to flower than it said on the seed packet, but they looked stunning and the bees adored them.

Perovskia atriplicifolia 'Little Spire'

Perovskia

(per-*ov*-skee-a) Common name – Russian sage) (Family – Lamiaceae)

Type of plant	Hardy, deciduous
Height/Spread	Up to 1.2m/1m
Flowers/Foliage	Long, narrow panicles of tiny, tubular, violet-blue flowers in late summer and autumn/Aromatic, deeply cut, ovate, grey – (almost white) green leaves
Best growing conditions	Sun; moderately fertile, free-draining soil
Longevity	Approximately 5 years
Propagation	Cuttings, spring
Maintenance/Problems	Cut back to permanent framework in spring/Usually trouble-free
Good for	Bees, butterflies, cutting
Looks good with	*Geranium*, *Phlox*, *Echinacea*, *Verbena*
Selected varieties/cvs	*Perovskia atriplicifolia* 'Blue Spire'* – violet-blue; *P. atriplicifolia* 'Little Spire' – violet-blue

Perovskia is technically a sub-shrub (a plant that is woody at the base but whose terminal shoots die back in winter) but it is often classified as a herbaceous perennial because that's how most people use it – including me.

Despite its common name, Russian sage is not edible, although anecdotal evidence suggests that you can eat the flowers. I think it is called 'sage' simply because it has some similar characteristics: it has grey-green, aromatic leaves and spikes of violet-blue flowers. (Actually I think it looks more like lavender.) The 'Russian' bit is easier to explain. It is named after the Russian Count (formerly General) Vasily Alekseevich Perovski, who introduced it to European gardens from what is now part of Kazakhstan, in the 19th century. So although it is called 'Russian', this has nothing to do with its geographical origins.

Planted individually, *Perovskia* has little impact, although it is a good foil for other more ostentatious plants. See them in a swathe, however, and the bluish haze of flowers seems to float above the almost white foliage, adding an almost otherworldliness to the border, especially in fading, evening light.

Perovskia atriplicifolia 'Blue Spire' can reach well over a metre in height; if you have a more modest space to fill, try *P. atriplicifolia* 'Little Spire', which has all the attributes of its big brother, but stands at just 60cm tall.

Persicaria affinis 'Darjeeling Red'

Persicaria bistorta 'Superba'

Persicaria

(per-sik-*air*-ee-a) (Common name – Bistort, Knotweed) (Family – Polygonaceae)

Type of plant	Hardy, deciduous
Height/Spread	Up to 1.2m/60cm
Flowers/Foliage	Spikes of tiny, bell- or cup-shaped white, pink or red flowers in summer into autumn/Clumps of dock-like oval green leaves
Best growing conditions	Sun or part shade; moist soil
Longevity	Approximately 4 years
Propagation	Division, spring or autumn
Maintenance/Problems	Tidy up in autumn/Usually trouble-free
Good for	Bees, cutting, ground cover (some species)
Looks good with	*Helenium*, *Anemone*, *Allium*,
Selected varieties/cvs	*Persicaria amplexicaulis* 'Firedance' – salmon red; *P. bistorta* 'Superba'* – pale pink; *P. bistorta* 'Hohe Tatra' – reddish pink; *P. affinis* 'Darjeeling Red' – pink flowers, red stems
☠ **BEWARE** ☠	Can cause skin irritation

It is unfortunate that one of the common names of *Persicaria* is knotweed, which immediately brings to mind the infamous Japanese knotweed, scourge of gardens and countryside alike, and now illegal to grow. This belongs to a different genus, so try and forget any prejudice you might have and come anew to *Persicaria*.

It is true that some species of *Persicaria*, such as *P. wallichii*, can be invasive to the point of being Triffidly troublesome, but choose your plants with care and there should be no problem. Go for *P. amplexicaulis* or *P. bistorta* and you will have spreading clumps, ideal for ground cover, which can easily be restrained by digging up any that outgrow their allocated space.

Probably the most readily available is *P. bistorta* 'Superba' – most garden centres seem to stock it – but I particularly like *P. amplexicaulis* 'Firedance', a relatively new introduction by Dutch nurseryman Piet Oudolf. It's more modest in its demeanour than some and has the most attractive salmon-red flowers. You will have to go to a specialist nursery to get it, but it's well worth the effort, I would say.

Phlomis longifolia

Phlomis russeliana

Phlomis

(*flo*-miss) (Common name – none) (Family – Lamiaceae)

Type of plant	Hardy, deciduous
Height/Spread	Up to 1.2m/80cm
Flowers/Foliage	Spaced whorls of lipped pink or yellow flowers in summer/Heart-shaped, felted green leaves
Best growing conditions	Sun; well-drained soil
Longevity	Approximately 4 years
Propagation	Division, spring; softwood cuttings, summer
Maintenance/Problems	Leave flower stems over winter, tidy up in spring/Usually trouble-free
Good for	Bees, cutting, winter interest
Looks good with	*Penstemon, Allium, Aconitum, Achillea, Geranium*
Selected varieties/cvs	*Phlomis russeliana** – canary yellow; *P. cashmeriana* – pale pink; *P. tuberosa* 'Amazone' – purple-pink, *P. tuberosa* 'Bronze Flamingo' – pinky-lilac flowers, red-bronze stems

I always think that the pink varieties of *Phlomis* look like 'wedding cake', many-tiered versions of *Monarda*, which is one reason why I wonder they are not more widely grown – people love a bargain and with this plant you certainly get more flowers for your money!

Some species, like the yellow-flowered *Phlomis* 'Edward Bowles' or *P. longifolia*, aren't actually perennials but nevertheless don't look out of place. If you want to keep your border true to its perennial roots, though, opt for *P. cashmeriana*, *P. tuberosa*, or *P. russeliana.* They all make excellent garden plants – *P. tuberosa* 'Amazone' planted with the toning *Allium* 'Purple Sensation' is particularly eye-catching, as is *P. russeliana* with *Geranium* 'Johnson's Blue'. And if you leave the tidying up until spring you benefit from the faded, but still attractive, stems during the winter: this is a plant that 'dies well', as the saying goes.

Phlox sp.

Phlox paniculata 'Blue Paradise'

Phlox

(floks) (Common name – none) (Family – Polemoniaceae)

Type of plant	Hardy, deciduous
Height/Spread	Up to 1.2m/60cm
Flowers/Foliage	Flat-faced, tubular, often fragrant flowers in a variety of colours in summer and early autumn/Opposite, lance-shaped, slightly toothed green leaves
Best growing conditions	Sun; moisture retentive but well-drained soil
Longevity	Approximately 3 years
Propagation	Cuttings, spring and early summer; root cuttings dormant season
Maintenance/Problems	Benefits from the 'Chelsea chop' (see Glossary, page 228); deadhead regularly; may need support/Powdery mildew; eelworm
Good for	Cutting
Looks good with	*Heuchera*, *Veronica*, *Geranium*, *Eryngium*
Selected varieties/cvs	*Phlox paniculata* 'David' – white; *P. paniculata* 'The King' – deep purple-blue; *P. paniculata* 'Brigadier'* – salmon pink; *P. paniculata* 'Blue Paradise' – lilac

Phlox, like many other perennials, seem to wax and wane in popularity and sometimes there is no explanation for it. Often, however, there is a trait that can seal a plant's fate and the poor old *Phlox* has two – susceptibility to powdery mildew and eelworm. Plant breeders have been selecting specimens that show some resistance to the former, but be vigilant: just because they are classified as 'mildew resistant' doesn't mean that they won't succumb at all. As for the latter problem, eelworm live in leaves and stems of plants, not in the root, so if plants are propagated by root rather than stem cuttings, the little blighters can't be passed on. All we need now is for swathes of *Phlox* to be used in an award-winning Chelsea show garden and it will be in the top ten perennial plant list!

Although there are many species of *Phlox*, the most widely available, and therefore most widely grown, is *P. paniculata*. Within this species there are scores of cultivars, ranging from the fragrant white *P. paniculata* 'David' to the deep purple-blue of *P. paniculata* 'The King', with all shades of pink, blue and red in between, so whatever your colour scheme there is bound to be a *Phlox* that will fit in. What cannot be guaranteed is that the one you choose will be scented; I treat those that are as an added bonus rather than the assumed norm.

Polemonium 'Bressingham Purple'

Polemonium caeruleum f. *album*

Polemonium

(pol-ee-*mo*-nee-um) (Common name – Jacob's ladder) (Family – Polemoniaceae)

Type of plant	Hardy, deciduous (sometimes evergreen, depending on climate)
Height/Spread	Up to 90cm/30cm
Flowers/Foliage	Clusters of cup-shaped blue, white or pink flowers in summer/Mounds of offset, lance-shaped green leaflets
Best growing conditions	Sun or part shade; fertile, well-drained soil
Longevity	Approximately 3 years
Propagation	Division, spring or autumn; species by seed
Maintenance/Problems	Deadhead regularly; tidy up after flowering/Powdery mildew
Good for	Cutting, bees
Looks good with	*Knautia*, *Nepeta*, *Geranium*, *Geum*
Selected varieties/cvs	*P. caeruleum* – soft blue; *P. caeruleum* subsp. *caeruleum* f. *album* – white; *P. carneum* 'Apricot Delight' – pink; *P. reptans* 'Stairway to Heaven' – violet blue with cream and pink-edged leaves; *P.* 'Bressingham Purple' – pale lavender blue

I definitely think that variegated leaves either suit a plant or they don't. They can make it even more attractive, like a cherry a-top an iced bun, or they jar and you shake your head, knowing that try as you might you won't be able to see the beauty others see in them. I'm shaking my head now as I recall some of the variegated *Polemonium* I have seen. They just don't work for me, but to show there are no hard feelings, I have included one in the list of varieties above.

I like the straightforward *P. caeruleum* with its soft blue flowers and bright yellow stamens: its only drawback is that it can self-seed quite freely and you end up with plants in the oddest of places. *P. carneum* 'Apricot Delight' needs moist, but not boggy, conditions; although it might be difficult to establish, if it is happy it will repay you with beautiful pink flowers with apricot centres – well worth the effort.

And why is its common name Jacob's ladder? Look at the leaflets – they resemble an old-fashioned ladder where there was a central shaft with rungs on either side, and I'm sure there is a biblical reference to Jacob dreaming of a ladder from earth to heaven. The variety *P.* 'Stairway to Heaven' may well be another allusion to it – or it could equally be referring to the song by Led Zeppelin!

Polygonatum x hybridum

Polygonatum

(pol-ig-on-*ah*-tum) (Common name – Solomon's seal) (Family – Asparagaceae)

Type of plant	Hardy, deciduous
Height/Spread	Up to 1m/1m
Flowers/Foliage	Clusters of pendulous, bell-shaped white (but sometimes pink, red or yellow) flowers, held below the leaf in early summer/ Lance-shaped, alternate green leaves carried along the stems
Best growing conditions	Light shade; moisture retentive, humus-rich soil
Longevity	Approximately 4 years
Propagation	Division, spring
Maintenance/Problems	Tidy up after flowering/Sawfly; slugs
Good for	Shade, cutting
Looks good with	*Pulmonaria*, *Corydalis*, *Geranium*
Selected varieties/cvs	*Polygonatum* x *hybridum** – white; *P. odoratum**– white; *P. odoratum* var. *pluriflorum* 'Variegatum'* – white with cream-edged leaves
☠ **BEWARE** ☠	All parts of the plant are toxic

The only time I ever heard my granddad utter even the mildest of expletives was one day in early summer, many years ago, when we were walking around his garden. We had come across a cluster of what looked to me like green, arching twigs stuck in the ground. These, I realized much later, were what was left after the dreaded Solomon's seal sawfly had had a feast. It is the rapacious larvae that do the damage, munching their way through the foliage at a rate of knots. You can be equally industrious and pick them off, but you have to keep it up: a couple of days' neglect and you are back to square one. Or you can use a suitable insecticide, but take care not to zap any good guys in the process.

If your *Polygonatum* are thriving you can increase your stock still further by dividing them in spring. Make sure that each piece has at least one terminal bud, or growing point, otherwise you will have laboured in vain.

The most widely grown species is *P.* x *hybridum*, but another notable species is *P. odoratum*, which has several cultivars: one has double flowers, another has variegated leaves, and they all have scented flowers.

Potentilla 'Arc-en-ciel'

Potentilla

(po-ten-*till*-a) (Common name – Cinquefoil) (Family – Rosaceae)

Type of plant	Hardy, deciduous
Height/Spread	Up to 45cm/60cm
Flowers/Foliage	Strawberry-like flowers in yellow through to red from spring to autumn/Divided, or fingered, green, often hairy leaves
Best growing conditions	Sun; well-drained, moderately fertile soil
Longevity	Approximately 4 years
Propagation	Division, spring
Maintenance/Problems	Cut back to the ground stems that have flowered; tidy up in autumn/Usually trouble-free
Good for	Bees (single-flowered varieties)
Looks good with	*Achillea, Eryngium, Aquilegia*
Selected varieties/cvs	*Potentilla* x *hopwoodiana* – pale to dark pink; *P.* 'Yellow Queen' – double, yellow; *P.* 'Volcan' – semi-double, rich red; *P.* 'Blazeaway' – yellow-orange; *P. thurberi* 'Monarch's Velvet' – raspberry red; *P.* 'Arc-en-ciel' – double, orange red

Probably the most ubiquitous of the different kinds of *Potentilla* available is the shrubby, yellow-flowered *P. fruticosa*, beloved of landscaping schemes nationwide. However, we are looking at the herbaceous sort, which have an altogether softer demeanour, often lolling around, adding an informal, almost easy-going, touch to the front of the border.

The majority of plants produce simple, strawberry-like flowers that first appear in early summer and seem to go on appearing until autumn – a real value-for-money plant. The colours range from a pale creamy yellow to a deep, velvety red, with just about every shade in between, including some lovely pinks. My favourite is *P.* 'Monarch's Velvet', which has raspberry-red single flowers with a deep red centre – luscious.

There are also double-blossomed varieties with flouncy, tutu-like flowers, although these seem to me to be somewhat at odds with the plant's fairly modest character – a bit like a member of the *corps de ballet* being thrust into the part of *prima ballerina* and not being totally comfortable with it. One that does relish the role, however, is *P.* 'Yellow Queen', with lovely double or semi-double flowers – a plant worthy of its regal name.

Primula Harlow Carr hybrid

Primula veris

Primula sp.

Primula

(*prim*-u-la) (Common name – Primrose) (Family – Primulaceae)

Type of plant	Hardy, deciduous/semi-evergreen
Height/Spread	Up to 50cm/45cm
Flowers/Foliage	Individual or clusters of lobed single or double flowers fused into a tube in various colours in spring/Basal rosette of entire or lobed, sometimes hairy, green leaves
Best growing conditions	Dappled shade; well-drained but moisture retentive soil
Longevity	Approximately 4 years
Propagation	Division, autumn or after flowering; seed, depending on species
Maintenance/Problems	Tidy up after flowering/Virus infections; aphids; slugs; snails; vine weevil
Good for	Shade
Looks good with	They actually look best in swathes of the same plant
Selected varieties/cvs	Primula Harlow Carr hybrids; *P. vulgaris* 'Lilacina Plena' – double, lilac pink; *P. denticulata* var. *alba* – white; *P. japonica* 'Miller's Crimson'* – pinkish crimson
☠ **BEWARE** ☠	Can cause skin irritation

A brief entry such as this can hardly do justice to this varied and populous genus. It ranges from the simple yellow, spring flowering primrose (*Primula vulgaris*) and cowslip (*P. veris*) found in hedgerows and meadows to the tall, summer flowering Himalayan cowslip (*Primula florindae*) with its profusion of nodding flowers. In between are a raft of border perennial species and hybrids covering the entire colour spectrum in both single and double flower forms. These are divided into ten sections, each containing plants of similar form. For example, 'Denticulatae' are drumstick primulas with tight spherical heads; 'Proliferae' have spires of tiered flowers – the so-called candelabra primula. *Primula* aficionados are able to categorize plants at a glance, but I would need an expert guide to lead me through all the different forms.

Living in the north of England, I have to make special mention of the *P.* Harlow Carr hybrids. These are candelabra-style *Primula* that originate at the northernmost RHS garden, Harlow Carr in North Yorkshire. The swathes of plants bordering the streamside in late spring and early summer are a truly wondrous sight.

Pulmonaria sp.

Pulmonaria

(pull-mon-*air*-ee-a) (Common name – Lungwort) (Family – Boraginaceae)

Type of plant	Hardy, deciduous/evergreen, depending on species
Height/Spread	Up to 30cm/50cm
Flowers/Foliage	Funnel-shaped flower with 5 lobes in violet, blue, pink and white in late winter and spring/Rosettes of lance-shaped or oval, often spotty, hairy green leaves
Best growing conditions	Dappled shade; moderately fertile, moisture retentive soil
Longevity	Approximately 5 years
Propagation	Division, autumn or after flowering; root cuttings, dormant season
Maintenance/Problems	Tidy up after flowering/Virus infections; aphids; slugs; snails; powdery mildew
Good for	Shade, bees
Looks good with	*Helleborus*, *Euphorbia*, spring flowering bulbs
Selected varieties/cvs	*Pulmonaria* 'Blue Ensign' – deep blue; *P.* 'Sissinghurst White'* – white; *P.* 'Diana Clare'– violet blue; *P.* 'Dora Bielefeld' – pink; *P.* 'Cotton Cool' – pink and blue
☠ BEWARE ☠	The leaves can cause an allergic reaction in some people

Both the Latin name of *Pulmonaria* and the common name of lungwort are allusions to the plant's use by apothecaries. They followed the principle known as the 'Doctrine of Signatures', where plants that resemble various parts of the body can be used to treat disorders of that part of the body. In this case the shape of the leaf resembles a lung and the spots on the leaves a diseased lung. I would wager that a lot more harm than good was done by the administration of some of the potions.

Medicinal use aside, *Pulmonaria* makes a lovely garden plant, with its welcoming splash of colour from the flowers in the spring, followed by the clumps of interesting foliage. It can be a superb foil for part-shade-lovers later in the season.

My favourite is *Pulmonaria* 'Blue Ensign', with gorgeous blue flowers that not only complement a number of other spring flowers but are a useful food source for early bees. If you want one to brighten a shady spot you can do far worse than *P.* 'Sissinghurst White': along with, yes, white flowers, it also has silver-spotted leaves that are evergreen – attributes that make it well worth growing.

Ranunculus aconitifolius 'Flore Pleno'

Ranunculus sp.

Ranunculus

(ra-*nun*-kew-lus) (Common name – Buttercup) (Family – Ranunculaceae)

Type of plant	Hardy, deciduous
Height/Spread	Up to 60cm/30cm
Flowers/Foliage	Single (often double) buttercup flowers in yellow or white, in spring or summer/Basal clumps of toothed or divided green leaves
Best growing conditions	Sun or part shade; moderately fertile, moisture retentive soil
Longevity	Approximately 4 years
Propagation	Division, autumn
Maintenance/Problems	Tidy up after flowering/Usually trouble-free
Good for	Informal or naturalistic planting
Looks good with	*Astrantia*, *Anemone*, *Dicentra*
Selected varieties/cvs	*Ranunculus aconitifolius* 'Flore Pleno'* – double, white; *R. acris* 'Flore Pleno'* – double, yellow; *R. ficaria* 'Flore Pleno' – double, yellow; *R. ficaria* 'Double Mud' – double, cream
☠ BEWARE ☠	All *Ranunculus* are more or less poisonous

I wouldn't blame you for doubting my sanity for including an entry for *Ranunculus*, otherwise known as buttercup or celandine. Most people spend an inordinate amount of time trying to eradicate them from the garden, and here I am suggesting that they are a good garden-worthy plant. Don't have me carted off just yet, though: of all the perennial *Ranunculus*, I find the double or semi-double forms the most attractive and the least invasive (double forms rarely if ever set seed) – and they look as if they are supposed to be there!

My favourite would be *Ranunculus aconitifolius* 'Flore Pleno'. It has a long pedigree, being known in Britain way back in the 16th century. It is thought to have been brought from France by the Huguenots who were fleeing persecution and couldn't bear to leave their precious 'fair maid of France' behind. It was certainly our gain because it has been in cultivation here ever since.

Rudbeckia hirta 'Prairie Sun'

Rudbeckia fulgida var. *sullivantii* 'Goldsturm'

Rudbeckia

(rood-*bek*-ee-a) (Common name – Coneflower) (Family – Asteraceae)

Type of plant	Hardy, deciduous
Height/Spread	Up to 60cm/50cm
Flowers/Foliage	Daisy-like, yellow flowers with dark centres in summer and early autumn/Alternate undivided to lobed green leaves
Best growing conditions	Sun; fertile, moisture retentive, well-drained soil
Longevity	Approximately 5 years
Propagation	Division, spring; basal cuttings, spring; softwood cuttings, summer
Maintenance/Problems	Deadhead regularly; tidy up after flowering/Slugs; powdery mildew
Good for	Informal or naturalistic planting, cutting, bees
Looks good with	*Aster*, *Verbena*, *Perovskia*, *Salvia*
Selected varieties/cvs	*Rudbeckia fulgida* var. *sullivantii* 'Goldsturm'* – deep yellow; *Rudbeckia lacinata* 'Juligold' – yellow; *Rudbeckia fulgida* 'Early Bird Gold' – yellow

Another native of North America, *Rudbeckia* shares the common name of coneflower with *Echinacea*. The centre of the flower does indeed look like a cone, and the easiest way to tell them apart is to look at, and touch, the cone. *Echinacea* comes from the Greek *echinos*, which roughly translated means 'spiny'. The centre of *Echinacea* does feel slightly prickly or spiny, whereas the centre of *Rudbeckia* is much softer.

You may come across *Rudbeckia* with orange, yellow and/or reddish-brown flowers. These are invariably varieties of *R. hirta*, such as 'Prairie Sun' (pictured), which is less hardy than other species and usually grown as an annual.

Of all the recent introductions of hardy *Rudbeckia*, *R. fulgida* 'Early Bird Gold' is probably the most exciting. It starts to flower in early summer and will carry on until mid to late autumn, depending on the weather. This very long season provides the border with a steady anchor while other herbaceous specimens with shorter flowering periods drift by.

Salvia x *sylvestris* 'Tänzerin'

Salvia nemerosa 'Amethyst'

Salvia

(*sal*-vee-a) (Common name – Sage) (Family – Lamiaceae)

Type of plant	Hardy, deciduous
Height/Spread	Up to 60cm/45cm
Flowers/Foliage	Spikes of white, pink, blue or violet flowers in summer and early autumn/Lance-shaped, aromatic grey or green leaves
Best growing conditions	Sun; well-drained soil
Longevity	Approximately 4 years
Propagation	Softwood cuttings, spring
Maintenance/Problems	Deadhead regularly/White fly; some fungal diseases
Good for	Bees
Looks good with	*Achillea*, *Aster*, *Verbena*, *Rudbeckia*, *Echinacea*, *Echinops*
Selected varieties/cvs	*Salvia* x *sylvestris* 'Blauhügel'* – mid blue; *S.* x *sylvestris* 'Tänzerin'* – purple-blue; *S. nemerosa* 'Caradonna' – violet purple; *S. nemerosa* 'Amethyst'– lilac pink

There are so many species of *Salvia* (over 900) that it can be a little daunting to try to get to grips with them – a bit like being faced with 'pick and mix' sweeties and wondering which ones to choose. Life is made a little easier when it comes to hardy *Salvia* grown for the herbaceous border, though. (There are many annual or tender species, or those designated as herbs, that we are not concerned with here.) I say easier, but there is much confusion, even among experts; you will find a cultivar listed as a particular species in one nursery catalogue, and as a different one in another. The names of the varieties I have selected (above) are, as far as I can tell, the accepted designation, but don't be surprised if they differ depending on where you buy them from.

Whatever they are called, hardy *Salvia* are one of the most useful plants to have in the perennial border: they provide a good contrast in form to a host of other plants; they have a wide range of colours; they are easy to grow; and they attract no end of bees and other pollinating insects. They also have aromatic leaves, but some of these are not as appealing as the species grown as herbs (*S. officinalis*). For example, I had a white *Salvia* (a variety of *S.* x *sylvestris*, I think) growing near our patio for a couple of years which attracted various comments like, 'Do you mind if we sit over there in the shade?' and 'Is your cat incontinent?' Enough said.

Scabiosa columbaria subsp. *ochroleuca*

Scabiosa caucasica 'Clive Greaves'

Scabiosa

(skay-bee-*o*-sa) (Common name – Scabious, Pincushion flower) (Family – Dipsacaceae)

Type of plant	Hardy, deciduous
Height/Spread	Up to 60cm/30cm
Flowers/Foliage	Pincushion flowers in white, pink, blue or purple in summer/Basal, spear-shaped, slightly hairy green leaves
Best growing conditions	Sun; well-drained, alkaline soil
Longevity	Approximately 3 years
Propagation	Basal cuttings, spring; division, spring or autumn
Maintenance/Problems	Deadhead regularly; may need support; tidy up after flowering/Usually trouble-free
Good for	Bees, cutting
Looks good with	*Rosa*, *Penstemon*, *Verbena*, *Salvia*
Selected varieties/cvs	*Scabiosa caucasica* 'Clive Greaves'* – lavender blue; *S. caucasica* 'Goldingensis' – dark lavender; *S. caucasica* 'White Perfection' – white; *S. columbaria* subsp. *ochroleuca* – creamy yellow

Nearly all plants thrive in 'ordinary' neutral soil, but some plants will be happier in soil on the acid side, others prefer slightly alkaline conditions. *Scabiosa* belong in the last category. Having moved north, leaving Sussex and its chalky, downland soil behind, I sometimes yearn to be able to grow the magnificent specimens of *Scabiosa*, *Sidalcea* and *Dianthus* that congregate in my childhood garden memories. It's not that I can't grow them here in Lancashire, and no doubt nostalgia is playing an active part here, but they are weedy, sickly-looking things compared to those that I remember my dad growing on his nursery.

Probably the most well-known variety, and widest grown, is *S. caucasica* 'Clive Greaves' – this is certainly the one that Dad grew. The fact that it was launched in 1929 and is still going, and growing, strong says a great deal about its constitution and garden-worthiness.

Other varieties of note available include the white form *S. caucasica* 'White Perfection': I also like the creamy-yellow flowers of *S. columbaria* subsp. *ochroleuca*, of which there is a new, more compact form – *S. columbaria* subsp. *ochroleuca* 'Moon Dance'.

Sedum spectabile 'Brilliant'

Sedum 'Strawberries and Cream'

Sedum

(*see*-dum) (Common name – Stonecrop, Ice plant) (Family – Crassulaceae)

Type of plant	Hardy, deciduous
Height/Spread	Up to 60cm/50cm
Flowers/Foliage	Flat, terminal clusters of tiny star-shaped flowers in shades of pink in late summer and autumn/Alternate succulent green or grey-green leaves
Best growing conditions	Sun; well-drained soil
Longevity	Approximately 4 years
Propagation	Cuttings, spring and early summer; division, spring
Maintenance/Problems	Deadhead regularly; may need support; tidy up when seed heads become tatty/Slugs; snails; vine weevil
Good for	Bees
Looks good with	*Aster, Echinacea, Perovskia*
Selected varieties/cvs	*Sedum* 'Herbstfreude'* – deep pink; *S.* 'Strawberries and Cream' – dark pink and white; *S. spectabile* 'Brilliant'* – pink; *S. telephium* 'Purple Emperor'* – purplish pink with deep purple leaves

Sedum are archetypal plants for late summer and into autumn: there is barely a garden I have visited over the years that doesn't have at least one kind or another. And they certainly earn their keep: not only do they provide colour and interest in the border, but the copious nectar they produce is a magnet for pollinating and beneficial insects.

The only disparaging remarks I have heard about *Sedum* are those that bemoan the sometimes lax, floppy habit that can leave a gap in the centre of the plant. More often than not this is because plants have been too well fed and the stems have become soft, unable to hold up the heavy heads of flowers – ease back on the nutrients a little and they will toughen up. A friend of mine also pinches out the growing tip in early summer to encourage side growth: this results in smaller, lighter flower heads but there are many more of them, and the shorter stems are able to support them.

Sidalcea 'Sussex Beauty'

Sidalcea 'Wine Red'

Sidalcea 'Little Princess'

Sidalcea

(sid-*al*-see-a) (Common name – Prairie mallow) (Family – Malvaceae)

Type of plant	Hardy, deciduous
Height/Spread	Up to 90cm/45cm
Flowers/Foliage	Spikes of open, mallow-like flowers in white, pink or crimson in summer/Rounded lower leaves, divided leaves on the flowering stems
Best growing conditions	Sun; moisture retentive, well-drained soil
Longevity	Approximately 4 years
Propagation	Division, spring
Maintenance/Problems	Cut back stems after flowering to encourage new growth; taller cultivars may need support/Slugs; rust
Good for	Bees, cutting
Looks good with	*Nepeta, Echinacea, Echinops*
Selected varieties/cvs	*Sidalcea* 'Elsie Heugh'* – pale pink; *S.* 'William Smith'* – salmon pink; *S.* 'Little Princess' – pale pink; *S.* 'Sussex Beauty' – pink

Most gardeners tell me that *Sidalcea* need neutral to slightly acid soil, which seems odd to me because my dad used to grow gorgeous specimens on his slightly alkaline soil in Sussex. I remember them with fondness, especially the one with fringed edges to the pink petals, the flowers of which I used as fairy skirts for the 'ballerinas' I fashioned out of sticks tied with cotton. I discovered much later that this was *S.* 'Elsie Heugh', a cultivar that has been around since 1936 and is still popular.

A more recent introduction is *S.* 'Little Princess', which grows to a compact 40cm – much shorter than other cultivars, and so ideal for the middle or front of the border.

The majority of *Sidalcea* have pink flowers, but for something with a little more intensity the deepest colour I have come across is *S.* 'Wine Red'; as its name implies, it is the colour of red wine – more of a Beaujolais Nouveau than a full-bodied Syrah, but certainly the darkest to date.

Solidago rigida

Solidago

(sol-ee-*day*-go) (Common name – Goldenrod) (Family – Asteraceae)

Type of plant	Hardy, deciduous
Height/Spread	Up to 2m/1m
Flowers/Foliage	Spikes of dense sprays of small yellow flowers in late summer and autumn/Alternate, lance-shaped or elliptical toothed green leaves
Best growing conditions	Sun; moisture retentive, fertile soil
Longevity	Approximately 5 years
Propagation	Division, spring; basal cuttings, spring
Maintenance/Problems	Cut back stems after flowering/Powdery mildew
Good for	Insects, cutting
Looks good with	*Echinacea*, *Echinops*, *Aster*
Selected varieties/cvs	*Solidago* 'Goldenmosa'*; *S.* 'Goldkind'; *S.* 'Laurin'; *S. rigida* – all species and varieties are yellow

A gasp of disbelief went round the gardening club when I told them I had planted a *Solidago*. 'Crazy. I told you she was crazy, didn't I? Who in their right mind would plant one of *those*?' Needless to say, it is not a universally loved perennial. I include it here partly because it has stood the test of time, and partly to try to convince people that it is not the bullying thug that crowds out all its neighbours that is conjured up in so many minds.

I have, in fact, planted two cultivars: the compact *S.* 'Laurin', with deep yellow flowers, which grows to only 40cm; and *S.* 'Goldkind', which is clump-forming and reaches about 60cm – ideal for cutting. I also have *S. rigida*, which has uncharacteristic flat-topped clusters of flowers which the bees love.

As in other areas of aesthetics and culture, trends for cut flowers come and go. This is undoubtedly true of *Solidago.* Having worn the badge of undesirability for too many years, it has once again been recognized as a worthy cut flower, especially with the vogue for natural and informal arrangements. I saw it used prolifically in the church flowers for an autumn country wedding recently and it looked stunning.

Stachys officinalis 'Hummelo'

Stachys byzantina

Stachys

(*stak*-is) (Common name – Woundwort, Lamb's ears) (Family – Lamiaceae)

Type of plant	Hardy, mainly evergreen
Height/Spread	Up to 60cm/60cm
Flowers/Foliage	Spikes of tubular, lipped pink or purplish flowers in late spring to summer/Opposite elliptical green or silver, sometimes hairy leaves
Best growing conditions	Silver, hairy leaves: sun; well-drained soil; other leaves: sun or part shade; moist soil
Longevity	Approximately 4 years
Propagation	Division, spring
Maintenance/Problems	Tidy up in spring/Slugs; snails
Good for	Insects, ground cover
Looks good with	*Achillea, Verbena, Echinacea, Echinops, Heuchera*
Selected varieties/cvs	*Stachys byzantina* – grey-green foliage, pink flowers; *S. macrantha* 'Superba' – green foliage, deep pinkish-purple flowers; *S. officinalis* 'Hummelo' – green foliage, purplish-pink flowers

The *Stachys* that most gardeners are familiar with is *S. byzantina* or one of its cultivars. This is the evergreen, mat-forming species with grey-green, felted leaves that give it its common name of lamb's ears.

S. byzantina is a particularly useful plant if you have a dry, sunny spot in your garden. It hails from the Middle East (hence *byzantina*) where such conditions prevail and has adapted to survive. Its grey-green leaves reflect heat, and the dense coating of felt-like hairs trap any moisture that is available. Underground, the rhizomatous roots store water to help it through periods of drought. Certainly one to consider if we get even more hosepipe bans in the future.

I like *S. officinalis*, and its cultivar *S. officinalis* 'Hummelo' with spikes of deep, purplish-pink flowers. The name *officinalis* is an indication that the plant was used by apothecaries, who were the forerunners of physicians and doctors. Before modern drugs came along, the only relief for illnesses and diseases was plant-based remedies. When the Latin bi-nomial system of classifying plants was introduced, this medicinal use was recognized in the species name.

Thalictrum aquilegiifolium
Thalictrum flavum

Thalictrum

(thal-*ik*-trum) (Common name – Meadow rue) (Family – Ranunculaceae)

Type of plant	Hardy, deciduous
Height/Spread	Up to 1.5m/60cm
Flowers/Foliage	Dense, almost fluffy, clusters of tiny white, yellow, pink, mauve or purple flowers with prominent stamens in late spring and summer/Divided, lobed or toothed bluish leaves, often similar in appearance to Aquilegia or maidenhair fern
Best growing conditions	Sun; moist, moderately fertile soil
Longevity	Approximately 4 years
Propagation	Seed, autumn; divide shorter species, spring
Maintenance/Problems	Benefits from the 'Chelsea chop' (see Glossary, page 228); deadhead regularly; cut back in spring/Usually trouble-free
Good for	Bees, back of the border
Looks good with	*Geranium*, *Aster*, *Rudbeckia*, *Phlox*, *Aconitum*
Selected varieties/cvs	*Thalictrum delavayi* var. *decorum* – lavender; *T. aquilegiifolium* – lilac purple; *T. delavayi* 'Hewitt's Double'* – double, lavender pink; *T. flavum* – yellow; *T. tuberosum* – creamy white; *T. reniforme* – lilac pink
☠ BEWARE ☠	All parts of the plant are toxic if ingested; contact with foliage may cause irritation

Thalictrum often come into their own in a supporting role: their unassuming elegance may lack the 'wow' factor of some border divas, but they nevertheless add a touch of gossamer-like charm that enhances, and imperceptibly strengthens, the rest of the planting.

The most well-known species of *Thalictrum* are tall, making them ideal candidates for the back of the border, but there are some that reach little more than 60cm.

The most arresting display of *Thalictrum* I have seen was at RHS Harlow Carr. Describing this swathe of *T. flavum* in visual terms is perhaps the wrong way to go about it, because what drew me initially was the unmistakable thrum of bees. The plants were covered with bees of all kinds, the various earthy colours of their bodies contrasting with the pale yellow of the flowers: what a sight – and sound!

Verbascum phoeniceum 'Violetta'

Verbascum 'Cherry Helen'

Verbascum

(ver-*bass*-kum) (Common name – Mullein) (Family – Scrophulariaceae)

Type of plant	Hardy, deciduous
Height/Spread	Up to 1m/50cm
Flowers/Foliage	Spikes of 5-petalled flowers in a variety of colours including white, pink, yellow and purple in summer/Basal rosettes of soft, sometimes woolly, green leaves
Best growing conditions	Sun; well-drained soil
Longevity	Approximately 3 years
Propagation	Seed, autumn; root cuttings, dormant season; careful division, spring or autumn
Maintenance/Problems	After flowering, cut back main stem to encourage side flowers to develop; tidy up in autumn/Mullein moth; powdery mildew
Good for	Bees
Looks good with	*Campanula, Echinops, Gaillardia, Phlox*
Selected varieties/cvs	*Verbascum* 'Gainsborough'* – yellow; *V.* 'Cotswold Queen' – biscuit yellow; *V.* 'Jackie' – peachy pink; *V.* 'Cherry Helen' – dusky cherry red; *V. phoeniceum* 'Violetta' – purple-violet

Some of the flower colours of *Verbascum* almost defy description: many of them look as if they started out as vibrant watercolours but were inadvertently mixed with a dirty brush – there is an edge of subdual to them. Even Vita Sackville-West described them as 'dusty, fusty, musty'. But she also wrote that they looked as though 'a colony of tiny buff butterflies had settled all over them' – much more poetic and appealing.

Don't let the slightly murky colours of some of the cultivars put you off – there are others which, despite still lacking in vibrancy, have a soothing subtlety that makes them ideal companions to any number of other shades and tones.

The majority of *Verbascum* are short-lived (some, like *V. bombyciferum*, are even biennial, so it is as well to take root cuttings of favourite specimens. Be careful, though: some hybrids have Plant Breeder's Rights attached to them, which means that you are not allowed to propagate from them (see page 12). This will be clearly indicated on the plant label.

Verbena bonariensis

Verbena

(ver-*bee*-na) (Common name – Vervain) (Family – Verbenaceae)

Type of plant	Hardy (half hardy in some areas), deciduous
Height/Spread	Up to 1.5m/60cm
Flowers/Foliage	Clusters of small, tubed and lobed flowers in lilac, purple or violet from late spring/Narrow toothed, lobed or dissected green leaves
Best growing conditions	Sun; well-drained soil
Longevity	Approximately 3 years
Propagation	Seed, spring; softwood cuttings, spring
Maintenance/Problems	After flowering, cut back main stem to encourage side flowers to develop; cut back to 30cm in late autumn/Powdery mildew
Good for	Insects, cutting
Looks good with	Almost anything!
Selected varieties/cvs	*Verbena bonariensis** – lilac purple; *V. bonariensis* 'Lollipop' – lavender; *V. rigida** – purple; *V. hastata* – violet

There is little doubt that the most well-known member of the *Verbena* clan is *V. bonariensis*. Few gardens seem to be without this tall 'see-through' plant with stilt-like stems and clusters of tiny insect-attracting flowers. As long as it is happy with where you have planted it, it will repay you with dozens, if not hundreds, of seedlings: a blessing or a bane depending on which way you look at it. If you find the straightforward *V. bonariensis* just too tall and unwieldy, there is *V. bonariensis* 'Lollipop', a more compact version that will sit happily towards the front of the border.

There are, however, various species other than the one named after Buenos Aires that are every bit as garden-worthy. There is the much shorter-growing *V. rigida*, which, I have to say, can struggle with our northern winters unless I give it a good mulch. *V. hastata* has flowers that are held on spikes rather than in clusters: I find this one a little more hardy, unless it gets wet feet in the winter.

Veronica longifolia

Veronica spicata 'Fairy Tale'

Veronica

(ver-*on*-ee-ka) (Common name – Speedwell) (Family – Scrophulariaceae)

Type of plant	Hardy, deciduous
Height/Spread	Up to 1m/45cm
Flowers/Foliage	Spikes of tubular flowers with 4 or 5 petals in white, blue, purple, pink or red in summer/Lance-shaped or round, smooth or toothed green leaves
Best growing conditions	Sun; well-drained soil
Longevity	Approximately 4 years
Propagation	Division, spring or autumn; cuttings, spring or autumn
Maintenance/Problems	Cut back in autumn/Powdery and downy mildew
Good for	Cutting, insects
Looks good with	*Echinacea*, *Verbascum*, *Allium*, *Echinops*, *Campanula*
Selected varieties/cvs	*Veronica spicata* 'Romily Purple' – dark violet blue; *V. spicata* 'Fairy Tale' – pink; *V. spicata* 'Rotfuchs' – rose red; *V. gentianoides* 'Alba' – very pale blue; *V. longifolia* – lilac blue

There are many species of *Veronica*, including some that have become a veritable nuisance. *V. filiformis*, for one, was introduced as an alpine plant from the Caucasus in the 1830s and quickly escaped from its confines to become a real annoyance, especially in manicured lawns.

Disregard this type of *Veronica* and we are still left with a plethora of garden-worthy plants. Of all the species, my favourite is *V. spicata*. I like the small flowers held on tapering spikes, which attract no end of insects and seem to go on for ages; *V. spicata* 'Romily Purple' is particularly attractive, with its dark violet-blue flowers both contrasting with and complementing so many other plants in the border. A little further round the colour spectrum you will find *V. spicata* 'Rotfuchs'. Its name, which means 'red fox', might conjure up a rusty orange red colour, but it is in fact a magnificent deep rose red. I bought this plant before it was in flower, anticipating that its colour would be the yellow side of red; I planted it next to a bright yellow *Hemerocallis* – the result was, frankly, aarrggh!

Veronicastrum virginicum 'Pointed Finger'

Veronicastrum

(ver-on-ee-*kas*-trum) (Common name – none) (Family – Scrophulariaceae)

Type of plant	Hardy, deciduous
Height/Spread	Up to 1.8m/50cm
Flowers/Foliage	Branched spikes with small, 4-lobed flowers in white, pink or purple in late summer and autumn/Toothed, lance-shaped green leaves arranged alternately or in whorls
Best growing conditions	Sun or light shade; rich, moist soil
Longevity	Approximately 4 years
Propagation	Division, spring or autumn
Maintenance/Problems	May need support; cut back in spring/Powdery mildew
Good for	Cutting, drying, insects
Looks good with	*Echinacea*, *Rudbeckia*, *Aconitum*
Selected varieties/cvs	*Veronicastrum virginicum* 'Lavendelturm' – lavender; *V. virginicum* 'Spring Dew' – white; *V. virginicum* f. *roseum* 'Pink Glow' – pale pink; *V. virginicum* 'Pointed Finger' – lavender blue

The only species of *Veronicastrum* that you are likely to find in a nursery or garden centre is *V. virginicum*. This is the one that has a distinctive arrangement of foliage: three to six lance-shaped leaves set in whorls up the stems just below where the flowerheads emerge. So if you get your *Veronica* (which has similar-shaped flowers) confused with your *Veronicastrum*, this is the identifying feature to look for.

Although they belong to the same family – Scrophulariaceae – *Veronicastrum* are a quite different genus from *Veronica*. Tradition has it that it is named after St Veronica, with the addition of *astrum* meaning 'star', referring to the arrangement of leaves around the stem.

Its pastel colours are a welcome addition to the late summer and autumn border, which is often dominated by reds, yellows and oranges. I planted *V. virginicum* 'Lavendelturm' alongside *Aconitum* 'Bressingham Spire' and behind *Echinacea* 'Harvest Moon' – it looks pretty good, even though I say so myself!

Viola 'Etain'

Viola tricolor

Viola

(*vi*-o-la) (Common name – Violet) (Family – Violaceae)

Type of plant	Hardy, deciduous
Height/Spread	Up to 15cm/30cm
Flowers/Foliage	Violet-shaped flowers in colours that vary from white, to yellow, to pink and violet during various seasons/Heart-shaped, often toothed leaves
Best growing conditions	Sun or partial shade; fertile, neutral or slightly alkaline soil
Longevity	Approximately 3 years
Propagation	Division, spring or autumn; softwood cuttings, spring
Maintenance/Problems	Deadhead regularly/Powdery mildew; downy mildew; aphids; slugs; snails; grey mould; rust
Good for	Front of the border
Looks good with	*Alchemilla*, *Stachys*
Selected varieties/cvs	Too many to name: see below

Everyone knows what a *Viola* flower looks like – from the unmistakably scented, modest bloom of the sweet violet to the cheeky, sometimes brash visage of the pansy, they have a form that is like no other. These extremes are indicative of the huge range of plants that come under the genus *Viola*. Here we are concerned with perennial species, which for the most part include *Viola odorata* and its hybrids, and *V. cornuta* and its hybrids.

Probably the best-known *Viola* of all is *V. odorata*, the beautifully scented, violet-flowered species. I remember that it used to grow at the foot of the flint wall surrounding our parish church where I lived as a child; on Mothering Sunday we were allowed to pick some to give to our mums after the service. A choice, and very old, hybrid of *V. odorata* is *V.* 'The Czar', with strongly scented, deep purple flowers and long stems.

The summer flowering *V. cornuta* has a number of garden-worthy hybrids, too; one of the best is *V.* 'Etain', which has strongly scented yellow flowers with an orange eye and lavender-violet border – just lovely. Another is *V.* 'Nellie Britton', with soft lavender-pink flowers. And I just have to include *V.* 'Rebecca' (my daughter's name) – it has creamy-white frilled petals, with a splash of lavender and violet, and a suggestion of lemon yellow on the lower petals.

Zantedeschia aethiopica 'Green Goddess'

Zantedeschia

(zan-ta-*dess*-kee-a) (Common name – Calla lily) (Family – Araceae)

Type of plant	Hardy, evergreen depending on climate
Height/Spread	Up to 90cm/60cm
Flowers/Foliage	Spathes of white in summer/Large, heart or lance shaped green leaves
Best growing conditions	Sun; humus rich, moist soil
Longevity	Approximately 4 years
Propagation	Division, spring
Maintenance/Problems	Remove spent flowers; tidy up in spring/Aphids; leaf spot
Good for	The 'wow' factor, cutting
Looks good with	*Astilbe, Brunnera*
Selected varieties/cvs	*Zantedeschia aethiopica* 'Crowborough'* – white; *Z. aethiopica* 'Glow' – white flushed pink; *Z. aethiopica* 'Green Goddess'* – white with green streak
☠ **BEWARE** ☠	All parts of the plant are toxic; sap may cause skin irritation

For our purposes there are two main groups of *Zantedeschia*: the species *Z. aethiopica* and its cultivars, and other species and hybrids. The first are pretty near evergreen and hardy in our climate: I grow *Zantedeschia aethiopica* 'Crowborough', which survives a Lancashire winter with very little attention other than a good mulch of well-rotted manure in the spring. I am also keen to get hold of *Z. aethiopica* 'Glow', a sport of 'Crowborough' that is apparently available at a number of nurseries in the UK.

The second group tends to be those *Zantedeschia* with coloured spathes and, sometimes, spotted leaves. These are inclined to be on the tender side and are often grown in pots so that they can be taken inside over the winter, or are treated as you would *Dahlia*, lifting them in the autumn to be planted out again the following summer. These *Zantedeschia* also require a much more free-draining soil than *Z. aethiopica* and will rot if you give them the same conditions.

If you can bear to cut them, they make a stunning addition to a flower arrangement.

Appendix 1
Main flowering season of selected perennials – in order of season

I think I should add the words 'A rough guide to the' before the title of this appendix (and also Appendix 2), since although we traditionally recognize early spring, for example, as being the months of March and April, plants are governed by day length and temperature: how many times have we reached Easter only to find the daffodils long gone – or are still enjoying *Aster* in December? Plants start and stop growing according to natural conditions, not an arbitrary date, so these appendices can only really be an approximate guide to flowering times.

Early spring

Bergenia
Brunnera
Doronicum
Epimedium
Euphorbia
Helleborus
Pulmonaria

Late spring

Ajuga
Anchusa
Anthemis
Aquilegia
Centranthus
Convallaria
Dicentra
Euphorbia
Iris – bearded
Lamium
Polygonatum
Primula (some)
Ranunculus
Veronica
Zantedeschia

Early summer

Acanthus
Achillea
Alchemilla
Allium
Campanula (some)
Centaurea (some)
Centranthus
Cirsium
Corydalis
Delphinium
Dianthus
Dierama
Digitalis
Erigeron
Geranium (some)
Geum
Hemerocallis
Heuchera
Iris – beardless
Knautia
Lamium

Leucanthemum
Lupinus
Lysimachia
Malva
Nepeta
Paeonia
Papaver
Persicaria
Phlomis
Polemonium
Primula (some)
Scabiosa
Sidalcea
Stachys
Verbascum
Viola (some)

Late summer
Aconitum
Agapanthus
Agastache
Alchemilla
Alstroemeria
Artemisia
Astilbe
Astrantia
Campanula (some)
Centaurea (some)
Centranthus
Clematis
Coreopsis
Crocosmia
Echinops
Eremurus
Erigeron
Eryngium
Eupatorium
Filipendula
Foeniculum
Gaillardia
Gaura
Geranium (some)
Helenium
Hosta
Lamium
Lathyrus
Lavandula
Liatris
Ligularia
Lobelia
Monarda
Origanum
Penstemon
Phlox
Potentilla
Salvia
Thalictrum
Verbena
Veronicastrum
Viola (some)

Autumn
Actaea
Anemone
Aster
Chrysanthemum
Dahlia
Echinacea
Kniphofia
Perovskia
Rudbeckia
Sedum
Solidago

Winter
Helleborus

Appendix 2

Main flowering season of selected perennials – in alphabetical order

	Early Spring	Late Spring	Early Summer	Late Summer	Autumn	Winter
Acanthus			✻			
Achillea			✻			
Aconitum				✻		
Actaea					✻	
Agapanthus				✻		
Agastache				✻		
Ajuga			✻			
Alchemilla			✻	✻		
Allium				✻		
Alstroemeria				✻		
Anchusa		✻				
Anemone					✻	
Anthemis		✻				
Aquilegia		✻				
Artemisia				✻		
Aster					✻	
Astilbe				✻		
Astrantia				✻		
Bergenia	✻					
Brunnera	✻					
Campanula (some)			✻	✻		
Centaurea (some)			✻	✻		
Centranthus		✻	✻	✻		
Chrysanthemum					✻	
Cirsium			✻			

	Early Spring	Late Spring	Early Summer	Late Summer	Autumn	Winter
Clematis				❁		
Convallaria		❁				
Coreopsis				❁		
Corydalis			❁			
Crocosmia				❁		
Dahlia					❁	
Delphinium			❁			
Dianthus			❁			
Dicentra		❁				
Dierama			❁			
Digitalis			❁			
Doronicum	❁					
Echinacea					❁	
Echinops				❁		
Epimedium	❁					
Eremurus				❁		
Erigeron			❁	❁		
Eryngium				❁		
Eupatorium				❁		
Euphorbia	❁	❁				
Filipendula				❁		
Foeniculum				❁		
Gaillardia				❁		
Gaura				❁		
Geranium (some)			❁	❁		
Geum			❁			
Helenium				❁		
Helleborus	❁					❁
Hemerocallis			❁			
Heuchera			❁			

	Early Spring	Late Spring	Early Summer	Late Summer	Autumn	Winter
Hosta					❁	
Iris – bearded		❁				
Iris – beardless			❁			
Knautia			❁			
Kniphofia					❁	
Lamium		❁	❁	❁		
Lathyrus				❁		
Lavandula				❁		
Leucanthemum			❁			
Liatris					❁	
Ligularia				❁		
Lobelia				❁		
Lupinus			❁			
Lysimachia			❁			
Malva			❁			
Monarda				❁		
Nepeta			❁			
Origanum				❁		
Paeonia			❁			
Papaver			❁			
Penstemon				❁		
Perovskia					❁	
Persicaria			❁			
Phlomis			❁			
Phlox				❁		
Polemonium			❁			
Polygonatum		❁				
Potentilla				❁		
Primula (some)		❁	❁			
Pulmonaria	❁					

	Early Spring	Late Spring	Early Summer	Late Summer	Autumn	Winter
Ranunculus		❁				
Rudbeckia					❁	
Salvia				❁		
Scabiosa			❁			
Sedum					❁	
Sidalcea			❁			
Solidago					❁	
Stachys			❁			
Thalictrum				❁		
Verbascum			❁			
Verbena				❁		
Veronica		❁				
Veronicastrum				❁		
Viola (some)			❁	❁		
Zantedeschia		❁				

Appendix 3

Perennials for different places and purposes

Below are some of my recommendations for plant groupings. They are merely suggestions and are not meant to be exhaustive lists.

Perennials for sunny sites

Achillea
Agapanthus
Alstroemeria
Artemisia
Aster
Centaurea
Centranthus
Crocosmia
Dahlia
Delphinium
Dianthus
Dierama
Echinacea
Echinops
Erigeron
Eryngium
Gaillardia
Geranium (some)
Helenium
Iris – bearded
Kniphofia
Lavandula
Nepeta
Papaver
Penstemon
Phlomis
Rudbeckia
Salvia
Stachys
Verbascum
Verbena
Veronica
Veronicastrum

Perennials for shady sites with moist soil

Aconitum
Actaea
Anemone (some)
Astilbe
Astrantia
Helleborus
Heuchera
Hosta
Polemonium
Polygonatum
Veronicastrum

Perennials for shady sites with dry soil

Bergenia
Brunnera
Euphorbia (some)

Geranium (some)
Pulmonaria

Perennials for dry conditions

Agapanthus
Artemisia
Dianthus
Dierama
Eryngium
Nepeta
Sedum
Stachys
Verbascum

Perennials for cutting

Acanthus
Achillea
Aconitum
Agapanthus
Agastache
Alchemilla
Allium
Alstroemeria
Anemone
Anthemis
Aster
Astrantia
Campanula
Centaurea
Centranthus
Chrysanthemum
Cirsium
Coreopsis
Crocosmia
Dahlia
Delphinium
Dianthus
Dierama
Echinacea
Echinops
Eryngium
Euphorbia
Gaillardia
Gaura
Helenium
Heuchera
Knautia
Lavandula
Leucanthmum
Lysimachia
Monarda
Paeonia
Penstemon
Perovskia
Persicaria
Phlomis
Phlox
Polemonium
Polygonatum
Rudbeckia
Scabiosa
Sidalcea
Solidago
Verbena
Veronica
Veronicastrum
Zantedeschia

When should you cut your flowers?

We have to remember that the flower is a plant's reproduction mechanism. It is there to attract pollinating insects, and, once pollinated, the seed will grow and the flower itself will die away. So if your flower is showing loose pollen, it is too late to cut it because its death knell has already sounded and it will have a very short vase life. Most species can be cut in the bud stage, as long as there is some petal colour showing, or just when the petals have begun to unfurl. Dahlias are the exception – only cut these when they are fully open, but before the pollen starts to loosen. Spiky flowers, like delphiniums, should be cut when about a quarter of the flowers towards the base of the spike are already open.

What time of day should you cut your flowers?

Morning or evening? There is quite a debate on this. Some people advocate cutting flowers in the morning because that is when they are most turgid. Others say that you should cut them in the evening because they have had all day to photosynthesize, have built up their store of carbohydrate and will therefore last longer in the vase. If you cut in the morning, be sure to do it after any dew has dried (any moisture left on the leaves and flowers can promote fungus) and before it gets too hot. If you cut in the evening, wait until it is cool. The choice is yours.

Perennials for bees and other insects

This list is by no means exhaustive, as you will find insects attracted to no end of other perennials. But if you want to plant some of these perennials specifically for insects, make sure that you choose those with single flowers. There is little or no food for pollinators in double flowers.

Achillea
Aconitum
Agapanthus
Agastache
Ajuga
Allium
Anchusa
Anemone

Anthemis
Aquilegia
Aster
Astrantia
Bergenia
Brunnera
Campanula
Centaurea
Centranthus
Chrysanthemum
Cirsium
Clematis
Coreopsis
Dahlia
Digitalis
Doronicum
Echinacea
Echinops
Erigeron
Eryngium
Eupatorium
Filipendula
Foeniculum
Gaillardia
Geranium
Geum
Helenium
Helleborus
Hemerocallis
Heuchera
Hosta
Knautia
Kniphofia
Lamium
Lavandula
Leucanthemum
Liatris
Lupinus
Malva
Monarda
Nepeta
Origanum
Papaver
Penstemon
Perovskia
Polemonium
Potentilla
Pulmonaria
Rudbeckia
Salvia
Scabiosa
Sedum
Sidalcea
Solidago
Stachys
Thalictrum
Verbascum
Verbena
Veronica
Veronicastrum

Appendix 4
Perennials that may be harmful

Listed here are those perennials among my selected 100 that may be harmful in some way. This shouldn't prevent you from including them in your planting scheme – they are all worth growing. What you should do, however, is treat them with respect and grow them purely as decorative or ornamental plants.

If the plant is listed as toxic, it doesn't necessarily mean that contact with it will be fatal or extremely hazardous. The majority of toxic plants have to be ingested to cause any ill effect, but some may cause skin or eye irritation.

Wise precautions are to position plants well out of the way of children, vulnerable adults and pets, always wear gloves when you garden, and never rub your eyes.

Aconitum	toxic; skin irritant
Actaea	toxic; skin irritant
Alstroemeria	skin irritant
Anchusa	toxic
Chrysanthemum	skin irritant
Convallaria	toxic
Delphinium	toxic
Dicentra	toxic
Digitalis	toxic
Euphorbia	toxic; skin and eye irritant
Helenium	toxic; skin irritant
Helleborus	toxic; skin irritant
Iris	toxic; skin irritant
Lobelia	toxic; skin irritant
Lupinus	toxic; skin irritant
Persicaria	skin irritant
Polygonatum	toxic
Primula	skin and eye irritant
Ranunculus	toxic
Zantedeschia	toxic; skin and eye irritant

Appendix 5

Index of common names of plants and their Latin equvalent

Common name	Latin name
African lily	*Agapanthus*
Angel's fishing rods	*Dierama*
Avens	*Geum*
Barrenwort	*Epimedium*
Bear's breeches	*Acanthus*
Bee balm	*Monarda*
Bellflower	*Campanula*
Bergamot	*Monarda*
Bistort	*Persicaria*
Black-eyed Susan	*Rudbeckia*
Blanket flower	*Gaillardia*
Bleeding heart	*Dicentra*
Bugbane	*Actaea*
Bugle	*Ajuga*
Bugloss	*Anchusa*
Buttercup	*Ranunculus*
Calla lily	*Zantedeschia*
Catmint	*Nepeta*
Cinquefoil	*Potentilla*
Columbine	*Aquilegia*
Coneflower	*Echinacea*
Coneflower	*Rudbeckia*
Cranesbill	*Geranium*
Day lily	*Hemerocallis*
Dead nettle	*Lamium*
Dyer's chamomile	*Anthemis*
Elephant's ears	*Bergenia*
Fennel	*Foeniculum*

Fleabane	*Erigeron*
Foxglove	*Digitalis*
Foxtail lily	*Eremurus*
Gay feather	*Liatris*
Giant hyssop	*Agastache*
Globe thistle	*Echinops*
Goldenrod	*Solidago*
Granny's bonnet	*Aquilegia*
Ice plant	*Sedum*
Jacob's ladder	*Polemonium*
Joe Pye weed	*Eupatorium*
Knapweed	*Centaurea*
Knotweed	*Persicaria*
Lady's mantle	*Alchemilla*
Lamb's ears	*Stachys byzantina*
Lavender	*Lavandula*
Leopard plant	*Ligularia*
Leopard's bane	*Doronicum*
Lily of the valley	*Convallaria*
Loosestrife	*Lysimachia*
Lungwort	*Pulmonaria*
Mallow	*Malva*
Masterwort	*Astrantia*
Meadow rue	*Thalictrum*
Meadowsweet	*Filipendula*
Michaelmas daisies	*Aster novi-belgii* and *A. novae-angliae*
Monkshood	*Aconitum*
Montbretia	*Crocosmia*
Mullein	*Verbascum*
Ornamental onion	*Allium*
Pink	*Dianthus*
Poppy	*Papaver*
Prairie mallow	*Sidalcea*

Primrose	*Primula*
Red hot poker	*Kniphofia*
Peruvian lily	*Alstroemeria*
Pincushion flower	*Scabiosa*
Plantain lily	*Hosta*
Queen of the prairies	*Filipendula*
Russian sage	*Perovskia atriplicifolia*
Sage	*Salvia*
Scabious	*Scabiosa*
Sea Holly	*Eryngium*
Shasta daisy	*Leucanthemum*
Sneezeweed	*Helenium*
Solomon's seal	*Polygonatum*
Speedwell	*Veronica*
Spurge	*Euphorbia*
Stonecrop	*Sedum*
Sweet pea	*Lathyrus*
Thistle	*Cirsium*
Tickseed	*Coreopsis*
Valerian	*Centranthus*
Vervain	*Verbena*
Violet	*Viola*
Windflower	*Anemone*
Wolfsbane	*Aconitum*
Wormwood	*Artemisia*
Woundwort	*Stachys*
Yarrow	*Achillea*

Glossary

Acid soil

Soil with a pH (potential of Hydrogen) value of less than 7.

Alkaline soil

Soil with a pH (potential of Hydrogen) value of more than 7.

Basal

Parts that grow from the base of a plant.

Basal cuttings

Cuttings taken from the young growth at the base of the plant. Remove a shoot, 6–8cm long, from the base of the plant. Trim off the bottom leaves, making sure that you do not damage the stem. Leave at least one pair of leaves at the tip of the shoot. Put the cuttings around the edge of a pot, or in individual modules, filled with gritty compost. Water, and either put in a propagator or cover with a plastic bag until new roots and top growth appears. Check periodically and water and/or remove failed cuttings if necessary.

Bract

A modified leaf at the base of a flower.

Chelsea chop

To cut down all or some of the growth of a plant in late May, to promote longer flowering later in the season.

Cultivars (cvs)

Cultivar is a contraction of 'cultivated variety' – a group of cultivated plants clearly distinguished by one or more characteristics (such as flower colour) and which retains these characteristics when propagated.

Deadhead

To cut off spent flowers.

Division

A method of propagation whereby a plant is divided into separate parts during the dormant season. This method is ideal for plants with a fibrous root system. Lift the plant, remove some of the soil and gently prise the root ball apart. You may need a knife or even a spade to do this. Make sure there is at least one growing point to each clump. Either put the clumps into pots or replant them in the garden, watering them in well.

Flower

The part of the plant containing the reproductive organs.

Frost-hardy

This means that the plant is hardy to –5°C.

Frost-tender

This means that the plant is hardy to 5°C.

Genus

A category of plant classification, consisting of a group of species.

Half-hardy

This means that the plant is hardy to 0°C.

Harden off

To acclimatize plants from an indoor to an outdoor situation. To harden off plants, take them outside for a couple of hours on the first day, then increase the amount of time over a ten-day period until they remain outside.

Hardy

This means that the plant is hardy to –15°C.

Herbaceous

Plants with non-woody stems.

Mulch

A layer of organic matter applied to the soil surrounding a plant to protect the roots from frost, conserve moisture, enrich the soil, or inhibit the growth of weeds.

Neutral soil

Soil with a pH (potential of Hydrogen) value of 7.

Perennial

A plant that lives for more than two seasons.

Rhizome

An underground, creeping stem that acts as a storage organ and produces leafy shoots.

Root cuttings

Segments of root that are taken from the plant during the dormant season, planted and from which shoots will grow. This method is ideal for plants with thick roots. Lift the plant and wash the roots. Select a pencil-thick root and cut it off close to the crown. Cut each root into 5–10cm lengths: make a straight cut at the upper end and an angled cut at the lower end. Put the cuttings around the edge of a pot, or in individual modules, filled with gritty compost, so that the straight cut is level with the top of the compost. Water, and either put in a propagator or cover with a plastic bag. Check periodically and water if necessary.

Semi-ripe cuttings

Cuttings that are taken from partially ripened but still flexible new shoots in mid or late summer. Remove a non-flowering shoot, 6–8cm long, from the plant. Cut the stem straight across, just below a leaf node, and trim off the bottom leaves, making sure that you do not damage the stem. Leave at least one pair of leaves at the tip of the shoot. Put the cuttings around the edge of a pot, or in individual modules, filled with gritty compost. Water, and either put in a propagator or cover with a plastic bag until new roots and top growth appears. Check periodically and water and/or remove failed cuttings if necessary.

Softwood cuttings

Cuttings taken from young, non-flowering shoots that have not yet started to ripen, in spring to early summer. The method is the same for semi-ripe cuttings, above.

Spathe

One or sometimes two large bracts that surround a flower.

Species

A category in plant classification, below genus, which contains closely related plants.

Stratification

The storage of seeds in either warm or, more often, cold conditions to break dormancy and aid germination.

Sub-shrub

A plant that is woody at the base, but whose shoots die back in winter.

Tuber

Thickened, usually underground, food storage organ derived from a root or stem.

Variety

The category of plant classification below species. The naturally occurring variant of a species.

Useful addresses and websites

Author's website

www.the beegarden.co.uk

Also see author's page on www.amazon.co.uk.

Royal Horticultural Society

80 Vincent Square, London SW1P 2PE

www.rhs.org.uk

The Garden Studio

151a Southport New Road, Tarleton, Preston, Lancashire PR4 6HX

Contact Tricia Brown: 01772 812672

www.thegarden-studio.co.uk

Specialist perennial nursery, open to the public.

Cotswold Garden Flowers

Sands Lane, Badsey, Worcestershire WR11 7EZ

www.cgf.net

Specialist nursery, open to the public and mail order.

The Hardy Plant Society

www.hardy-plant.org.uk

The Hardy Plant Society exists to stimulate interest in growing hardy herbaceous plants.

The Cottage Garden Society

www.thecottagegardensociety.org.uk

The Cottage Garden Society (CGS) is an informal and friendly society of about 5,000 members in many countries, though most are based in the UK. It brings together amateurs and professionals who share an enthusiasm for this type of gardening.

Index

IMain entry is shown in **bold**

Acanthus **15,** 214, 216, 221, 225
Achillea **17,** 25, 69, 73, 77, 107, 111, 115, 141, 143, 147, 149, 165, 171, 179, 189, 199, 214, 216, 220, 221, 222, 227
Aconitum **19,** 77, 109, 117, 133, 171, 201, 209, 215, 216, 220, 221, 222, 224, 226, 227
Actaea **21,** 215, 216, 220, 224, 225
Agapanthus **23,** 215, 216, 220, 221, 222, 225
Agastache **25,** 89, 91, 141, 143, 153, 215, 216, 221, 222, 226
Ajuga **27,** 214, 216, 222, 225
Alchemilla **29,** 41, 211, 214, 215, 216, 221, 226
Allium 17, **31,** 35, 37, 65, 85, 143, 157, 163, 169, 171, 207, 214, 216, 221, 222, 226
Alstroemeria **33,** 215, 216, 220, 221, 224, 227
Anchusa **35,** 214, 216, 222, 224, 225
Anemone 19, 21, 31, **37,** 111, 137, 153, 169, 185, 215, 216, 220, 221, 222, 227
Anthemis **39,** 55, 159, 214, 216, 221, 223, 225
Aquilegia **41,** 79, 115, 135, 149, 179, 214, 216, 223, 225, 226
Artemisia **43,** 215, 216, 220, 221, 227
Aster 25, 37, **45,** 109, 187, 189, 193, 197, 201, 215, 216, 220, 221, 223, 226
Astilbe 21, **47,** 145, 151, 213, 215, 216, 220
Astrantia 15, **49,** 63, 83, 185, 215, 216, 220, 221, 223, 226
Award of Garden Merit (AGM) *see* Royal Horticultural Society Award of Garden Merit (AGM)

Bergenia **51,** 53, 65, 81, 214, 216, 220, 223, 225
Brunnera **53,** 81, 87, 93, 119, 213, 214, 216, 220, 223

Campanula 39, 41, 49, **55**, 85, 101, 149, 161, 163, 203, 207, 214, 215, 216, 221, 223, 225
Centaurea **57,** 214, 215, 216, 220, 221, 223, 226,
Centranthus **59**, 214, 215, 216, 220, 221, 223, 227
Chelsea chop 117, 141, 173, 201, **228**
Chrysanthemum **61**, 215, 216, 221, 223, 224
Cimicifuga *see* Actaea
Cirsium **63**, 214, 216, 221, 223, 227
Clematis **65,** 215, 217, 223

common names 225-7
Convallaria **67,** 71, 214, 217, 224, 226
Coreopsis **69**, 215, 217, 221, 223, 227
Corydalis 67, **71**, 177, 214, 217
Crocosmia 45, 57, **73,** 117, 215, 217, 220, 221, 226
cutting flowers 222
cuttings
  basal 228
  root 230
  semi-ripe 230
  softwood 231

Dahlia 73, **75,** 117, 213, 215, 217, 220, 221, 222, 223
Delphinium 19, 39, 65, **77,** 133, 137, 161, 163, 214, 217, 220, 221, 222, 224
description of plants 9
Dianthus 41, **79**, 191, 214, 217, 220, 221, 226
Dicentra 53, **81,** 129, 185, 214, 217, 224, 225
Dierama **83**, 214, 217, 220, 221, 225
Digitalis 39, 41, **85**, 214, 217, 223, 224, 226
dimensions of plants 9
division 229
Doronicum **87,** 214, 217, 223, 226

Echinacea 25, 45, 51, **89,** 105, 133, 165, 167, 187, 189, 193, 195, 197, 199, 207, 209, 215, 217, 220, 221, 223, 225
Echinops 69, **91,** 141, 143, 155, 189, 195, 197, 199, 203, 207, 215, 217, 220, 221, 223, 226
Epimedium **93,** 214, 217, 225
Eremurus **95,** 103, 215, 217, 226
Erigeron 83, **97,** 214, 215, 217, 220, 223, 226
Eryngium **99,** 155, 157, 173, 179, 215, 217, 220, 221, 223, 227
Eupatorium **101,** 215, 217, 223, 226
Euphorbia 53, 95, **103,** 115, 183, 214, 217, 220, 221, 224, 227

Filipendula **105,** 215, 217, 223, 226, 227
flowering season(s) of perennials 214-15, 216-19
Foeniculum 35, 73, 75, **107,** 215, 217, 223, 225

Gaillardia **109,** 203, 215, 217, 220, 221, 223, 225

Gaura **111,** 215, 217, 221
Geranium 31, 33, 41, 53, 55, 57, 67, 89, 91, 95, 99, 103, **113,** 161, 163, 167, 171, 173, 175, 177, 201, 214, 215, 217, 220, 221, 223, 225
Geum **115,** 175, 214, 217, 223, 225
growing conditions 10

harden off 229
hardiness 12
  frost hardy 229
  frost tender 229
  half hardy 229
  hardy 229
harmful plants 11, 224
height of plants *see* plant dimensions
Helenium 25, 61, 73, 75, **117**, 147, 169, 215, 217, 220, 221, 223, 224, 227
Helleborus **119,** 135, 183, 214, 215, 217, 220, 223, 224
Hemerocallis 19, 23, 59, 77, **121,** 207, 214, 217, 223, 225
Heuchera **123**, 173, 199, 214, 217, 220, 221, 223
Hosta 21, 45, 47, 93, 105, **125,** 129, 215, 218, 220, 223, 227

Iris – bearded 35, 79, 83 **127,** 214, 218, 220, 224
Iris – beardless 105, **129,** 151, 214, 218, 224

June gap 57

Knautia 97, **131**, 141, 153, 175, 214, 218, 221, 223
Kniphofia **133,** 141, 147, 215, 218, 220, 223, 227

Lamium **135,** 214, 215, 218, 223, 225
Lamprocapnos *see* Dicentra
Lathyrus **137,** 215, 218, 227
Latin names 12
Lavandula 97, 127, **139,** 159, 215, 218, 220, 221, 223, 226
Leucanthemum 55, 85, **141,** 143, 215, 218, 223, 227
Liatris **143,** 215, 218, 223, 226
Ligularia 47, **145,** 215, 218, 226
Lobelia **147,** 215, 218, 224
longevity of plants 10

Lupinus 57, **149,** 215, 218, 223, 224
Lysimachia **151,** 215, 218, 221, 226

maintenance of plants 10
Malva **153,** 215, 218, 223, 226
Monarda **155,** 215, 218, 221, 223, 225
Montbretia *see* Crocosmia

Nepeta 17, 31, 33, **157,** 175, 195, 215, 218, 220, 221, 223, 225

Origanum **159,** 215, 218, 223

Paeonia **161,** 215, 218, 221
Papaver 63, 77, 85, **163,** 215, 218, 220, 223, 226
Penstemon 153, 163, **165,** 171, 191, 215, 218, 220, 221, 223
perennials
  for cutting 221
  for dry conditions 221
  for bees and insects 222
  for shady sites with dry soil 220
  for shady sites with moist soil 220
  for sunny sites 220
Perovskia 9, 17, 165, **167,** 187, 193, 215, 218, 221, 223, 227
Persicaria 145, **169,** 215, 218, 221, 224, 225, 226
Phlomis 15, **171,** 215, 218, 220, 221
Phlox 19, 155, 165, 167, **173,** 201, 203, 215, 218, 221
plant breeder's rights (PBR) 12, 203
poisonous plants *see* harmful plants
Polemonium 85, **175,** 215, 218, 220, 221, 223, 226
Polygonatum 67, 103, **177,** 214, 218, 220, 221, 224, 227
Potentilla **179,** 215, 218, 223, 225
problems with plants 10
propagation 10
Primula **181,** 214, 215, 218, 224, 227
pronunciation 12
Pulmonaria 51, 81, 87, 93, 119, 177, **183,** 214, 218, 221, 223, 226

Ranunculus **185,** 214, 219, 224, 225

Royal Horticultural Society Award of Garden Merit (AGM) 11
Rudbeckia 45, 73, 75, 89, 99, 133, **187,** 189, 201, 209, 215, 219, 220, 221, 223, 225

Salvia 17, 23, 31, 49, 59, 63, 69, 85, 101, 111, 187, **189,** 191, 215, 219, 220, 223, 227
Scabiosa **191,** 215, 219, 221, 223, 227
Sedum 111, 159, **193,** 215, 219, 221, 223, 226, 227
Sidalcea 191, **195,** 215, 219, 221, 223, 226
Solidago **197,** 215, 219, 221, 223, 226
spread of plants *see* plant dimensions
Stachys **199,** 211, 215, 219, 220, 221, 223, 226, 227
stratification 231

Thalictrum **201,** 215, 219, 223, 226
toxic plants *see* harmful plants

Verbascum 35, 39, 55, 69, 89, 91, 99, 133, 155, 157, **203,** 207, 215, 219, 220, 221, 223, 226
Verbena 37, 63, 89, 91, 97, 99, 167, 187, 189, 191, 199, **205,** 215, 219, 220, 221, 223, 227
Veronica 173, **207,** 209, 214, 219, 220, 221, 223, 227
Veronicastrum 19, 101, 107, **209,** 215, 219, 220, 221, 223
Viola **211,** 215, 219, 227

Zantedeschia 129, 145, **213,** 214, 219, 221, 224, 225

OTHER BOOKS BY MAUREEN LITTLE

PLANTS AND PLANTING PLANS FOR A BEE GARDEN

How to design beautiful borders that will attract bees

This book will enable you to select bee-friendly plants, and to plan borders which are beneficial to bees, encouraging these most valuable of insects to come to your garden over and over again, both for sustenance and to aid pollination. It contains a wide range of practical, beautiful and easy-to-follow planting plans for bee-friendly gardens of all sizes, including: traditional mixed, cottage- and colour-themed borders; 'designer' and 'natural' borders; borders for acid and alkaline soils; ideas for container planting. It also includes over 180 colour illustrations.

£14.99 978-1-905862-80-1

THE BEE GARDEN

How to create or adapt a garden to attract and nurture bees

Bees play a vital and irreplaceable role in pollinating our flowers, fruit and vegetables. The more bees in your garden the healthier, more productive and more pleasant a place it will be. Yet bees are declining rapidly and many people, even if they do not wish to keep bees themselves, are asking what can be done on an individual basis to help the bee. This fully illustrated book is a response to that request. It will demonstrate in one accessible volume how each of us can play our part in providing a bee-friendly environment, no matter how much gardening space and/or time we may have.

£16.99 978-1-905862-59-7

THE KITCHEN HERB GARDEN

A seasonal guide to growing, cooking and using culinary herbs

This illustrated book will enable you to enjoy cultivating a kitchen herb garden and using its fresh home-grown herbs in your cooking. There is detailed information on how to plan, plant, grow and maintain thirty selected herbs, together with over sixty delicious recipes – from soups to sauces – for using herbs in your kitchen. You'll also find information on:

Using herbs to flavour oils, vinegars, butters, sugars and jellies
How to harvest, dry and preserve your herbs
How to grow herbs in containers
How to match herbs to ingredients in your cooking

£14.99 978-1-905862-89-4